4-14

BRODY'S GHOST ™

BRODY'S GHOST ™

BOOK 4

STORY AND ART BY
MARK CRILLEY

DARK HORSE BOOKS

Publisher - Mike Richardson
Designer - Justin Couch
Assistant Editor - Jemiah Jefferson
Editor - Rachel Edidin
Special thanks to Dave Land

Published by Dark Horse Books
A division of Dark Horse Comics, Inc.
10956 SE Main Street
Milwaukie, OR 97222

DarkHorse.com

To find a comic shop in your area call the Comic Shop Locator Service toll-free at (888) 266-4226
International Licensing: (503) 905-2377

First edition: April 2013
ISBN 978-1-61655-129-2

BRODY'S GHOST BOOK 4

10 9 8 7 6 5 4 3 2 1

Printed in the U.S.A.

THIS BOOK IS DEDICATED TO IAN JACKSON,
WHO REALLY MEANT IT WHEN HE SAID,
"LET'S STAY IN TOUCH."

THE STORY SO FAR...

Brody is a young man living in a decaying city a number of de-
cades from now. After being dumped by his girlfriend Nicole, he
allowed his life to spiral into a directionless mess. One afternoon
he finds himself face to face with the ghost of a teenage girl,
Talia, who tells him that she died of leukemia five years ago,
but that she won't be allowed into heaven until she unmasks
a serial killer known as the Penny Murderer and brings him to
justice. Reluctantly, Brody agrees to help. Talia leads Brody into
the dwelling of the ghost of an ancient samurai, Kagemura, who
trains Brody in body and mind in order to gain the use of Brody's
latent psychic abilities.

Once Brody gains great physical stamina and strength as well as
the ability to control his telekinetic powers, he takes it upon himself to bring down some of the city's most dangerous criminals,
attempting to get closer to the mystery of the Penny Murderer.
Talia has some ideas of her own—and sends Brody undercover
to speak to the victims' families and make physical contact with
their belongings. To his horror, Brody finds that he can make a
psychic connection, not only with the murder victims, but with
the murderer himself—and that Talia hasn't been entirely honest
about her own mode of death . . .

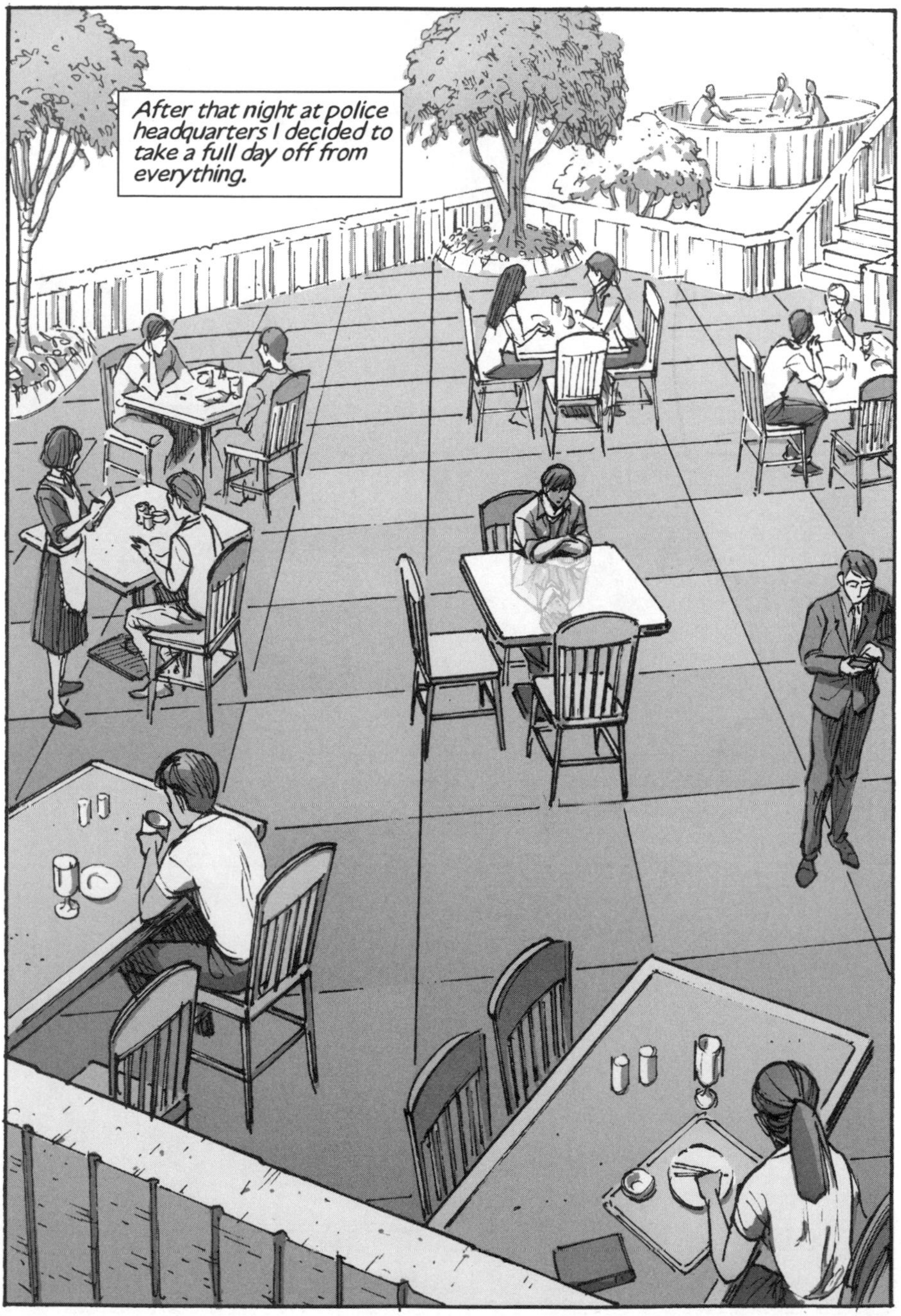
After that night at police headquarters I decided to take a full day off from everything.

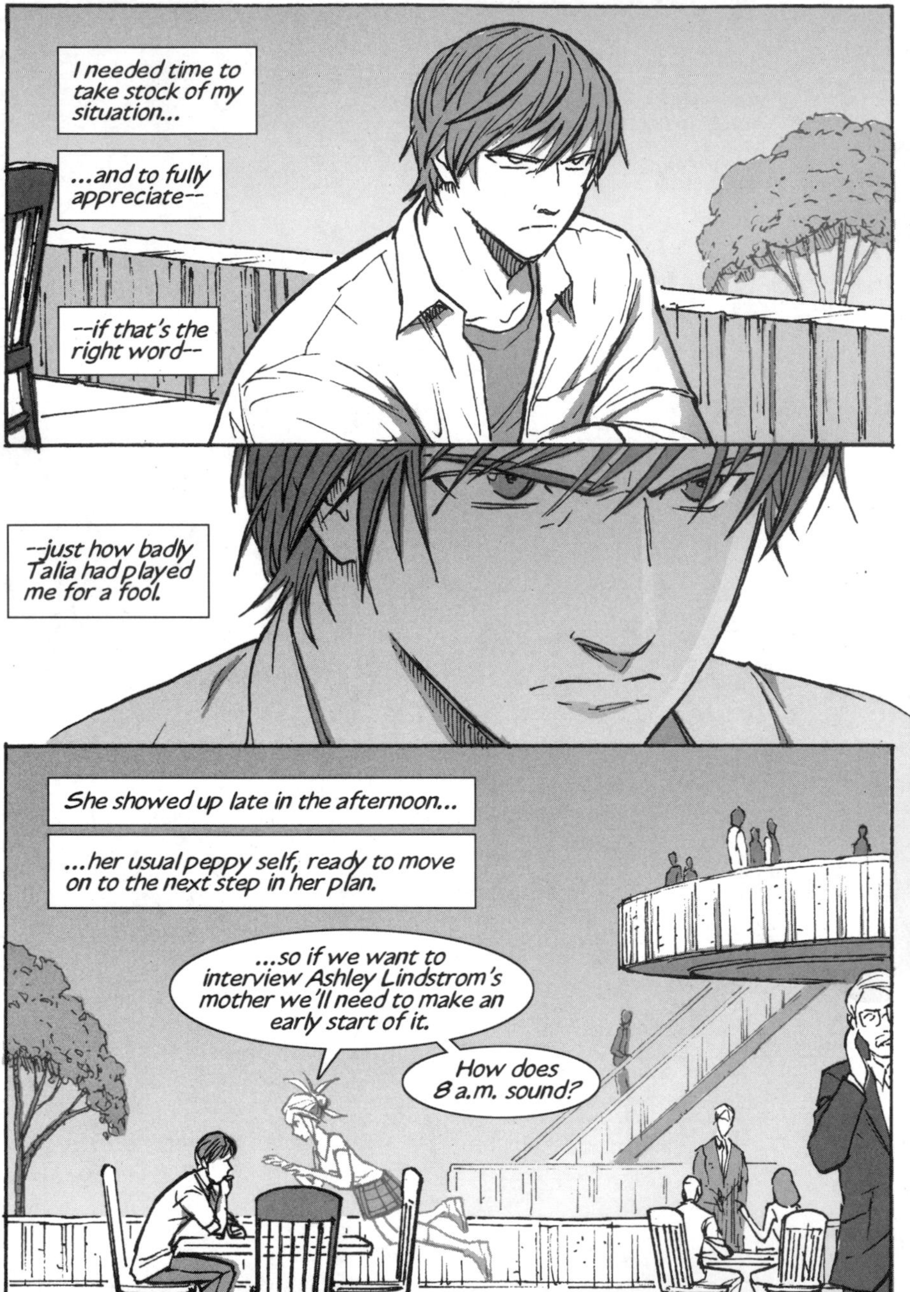
I needed time to take stock of my situation...
...and to fully appreciate--
--if that's the right word--
--just how badly Talia had played me for a fool.
She showed up late in the afternoon...
...her usual peppy self, ready to move on to the next step in her plan.
...so if we want to interview Ashley Lindstrom's mother we'll need to make an early start of it.
How does 8 a.m. sound?

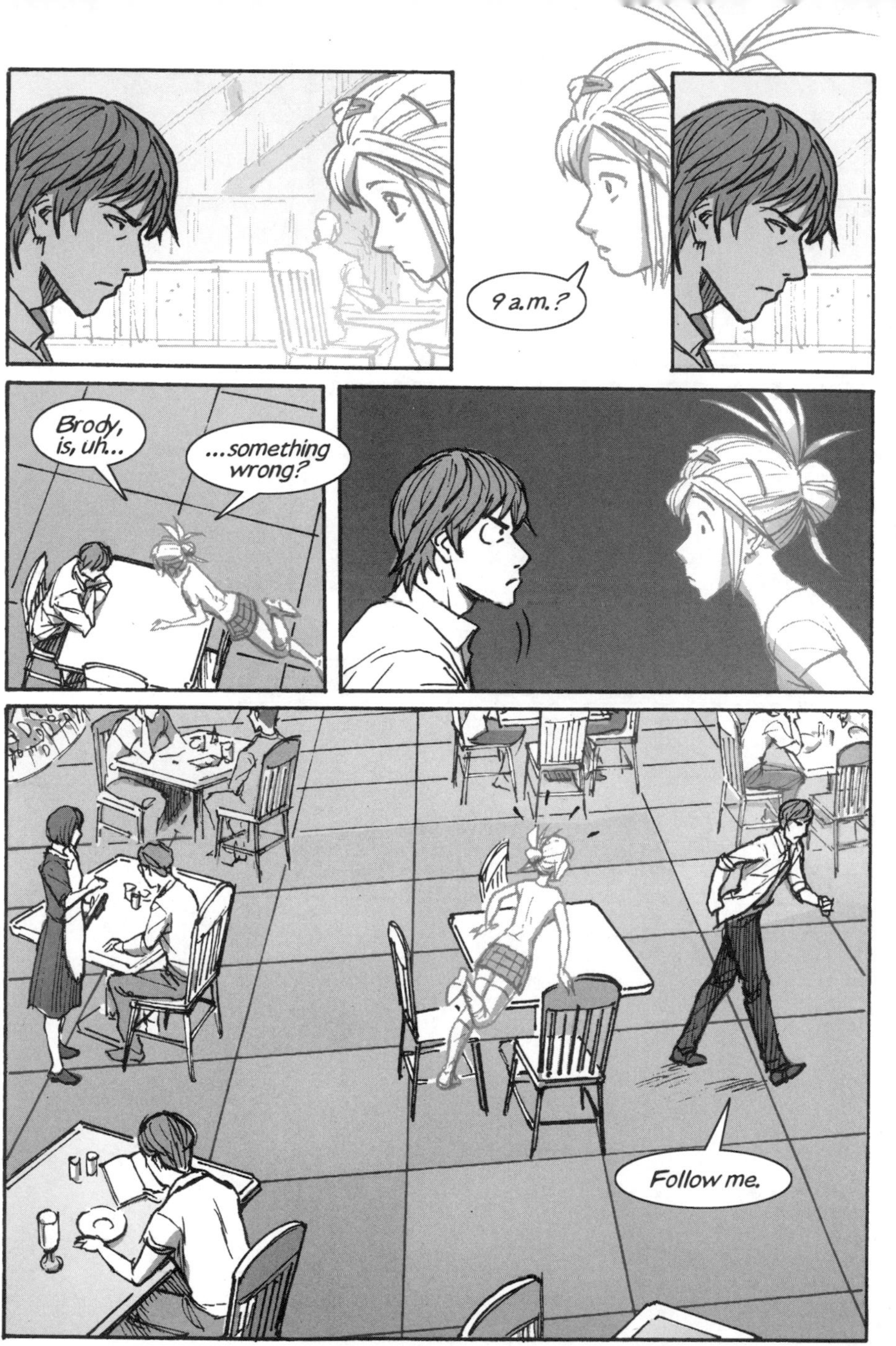
9 a.m.?
Brody, is, uh...
...something wrong?
Follow me.

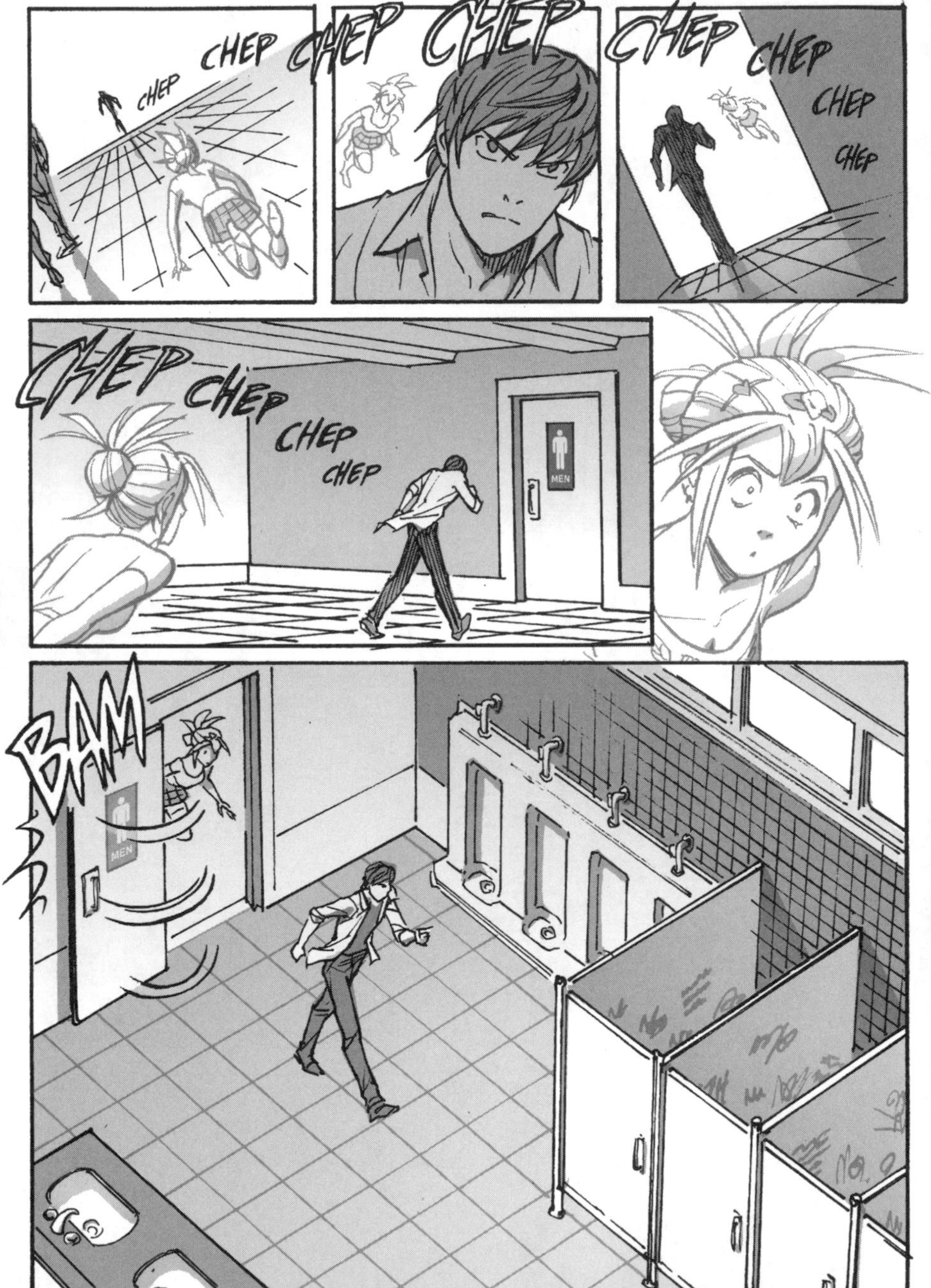
CHEP
CHEP
CHEP
CHEP
CHEP
CHEP
CHEP
CHEP
CHEP
CHEP
CHEP
CHEP
MEN
BAM
MEN

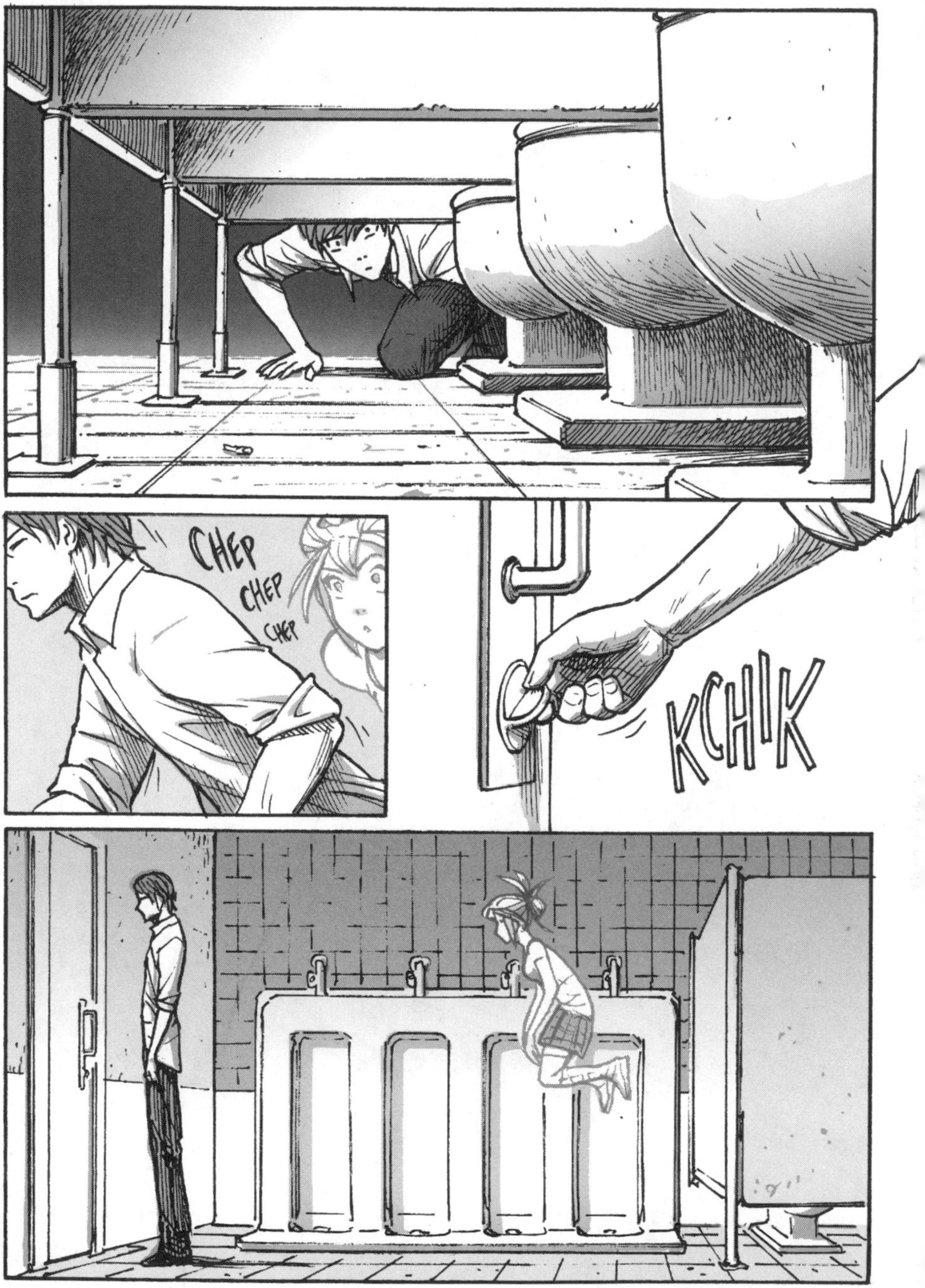
CHEP
CHEP
CHEP
KCHIK

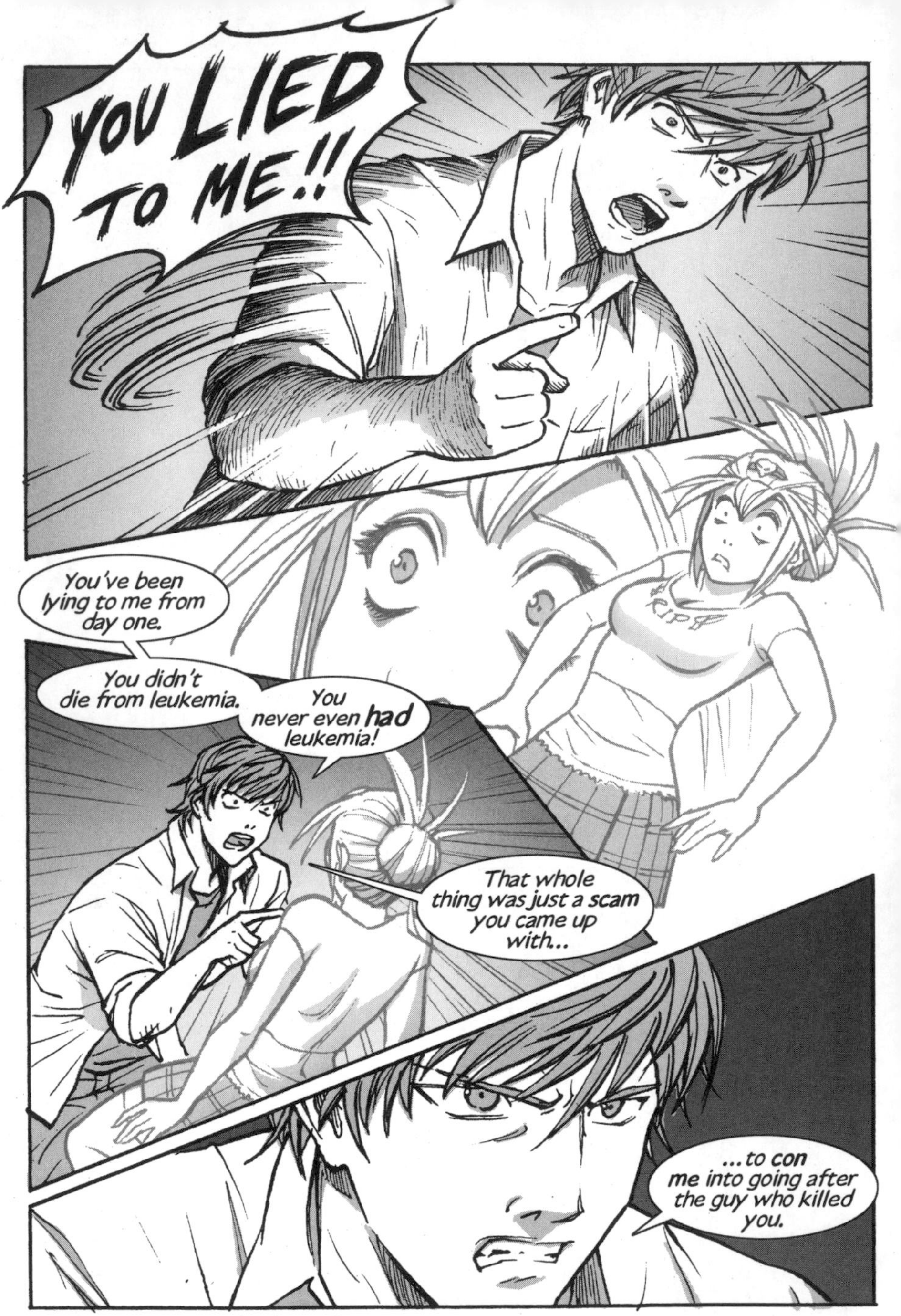
YOU LIED TO ME!!
You've been lying to me from day one.
You didn't die from leukemia.
You never even had leukemia!
That whole thing was just a scam you came up with...
...to con me into going after the guy who killed you.

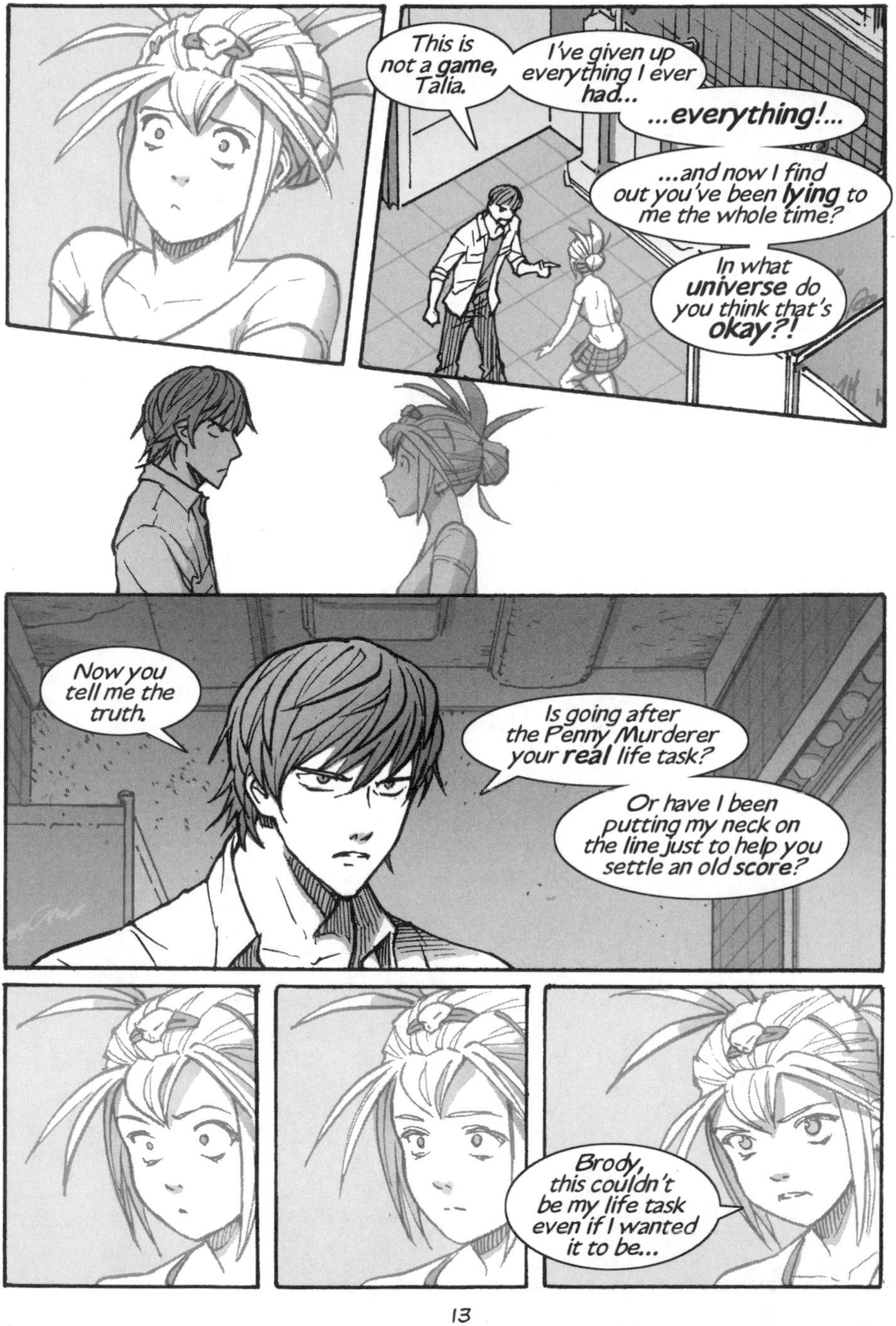
This is not a game, Talia.
I've given up everything I ever had...
...everything!...
...and now I find out you've been lying to me the whole time?
In what universe do you think that's okay?!
Now you tell me the truth.
Is going after the Penny Murderer your real life task?
Or have I been putting my neck on the line just to help you settle an old score?
Brody, this couldn't be my life task even if I wanted it to be...

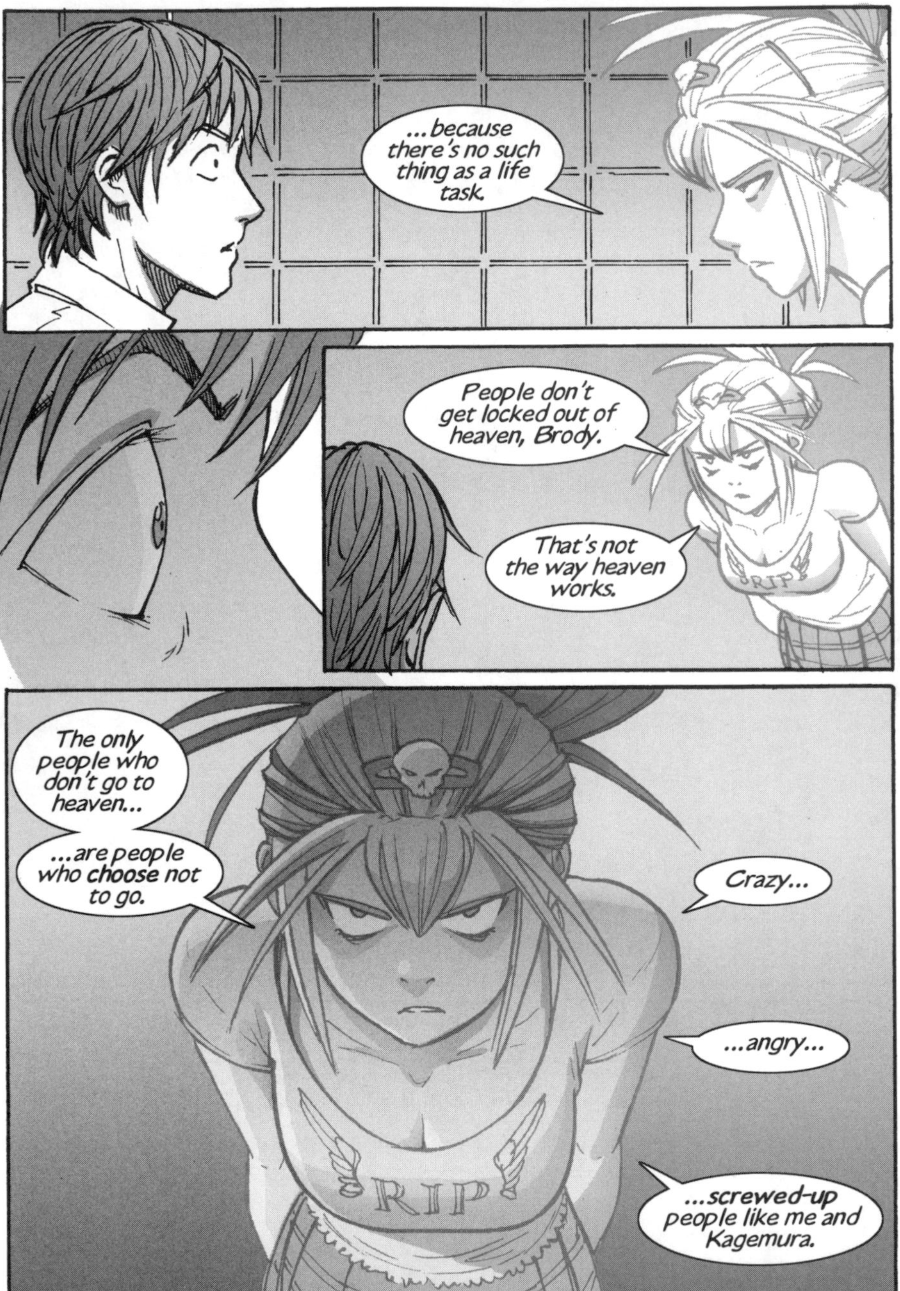
...because there's no such thing as a life task.
People don't get locked out of heaven, Brody.
That's not the way heaven works.
RIP
The only people who don't go to heaven...
...are people who **choose** not to go.
Crazy...
...angry...
...**screwed-up** people like me and Kagemura.
RIP

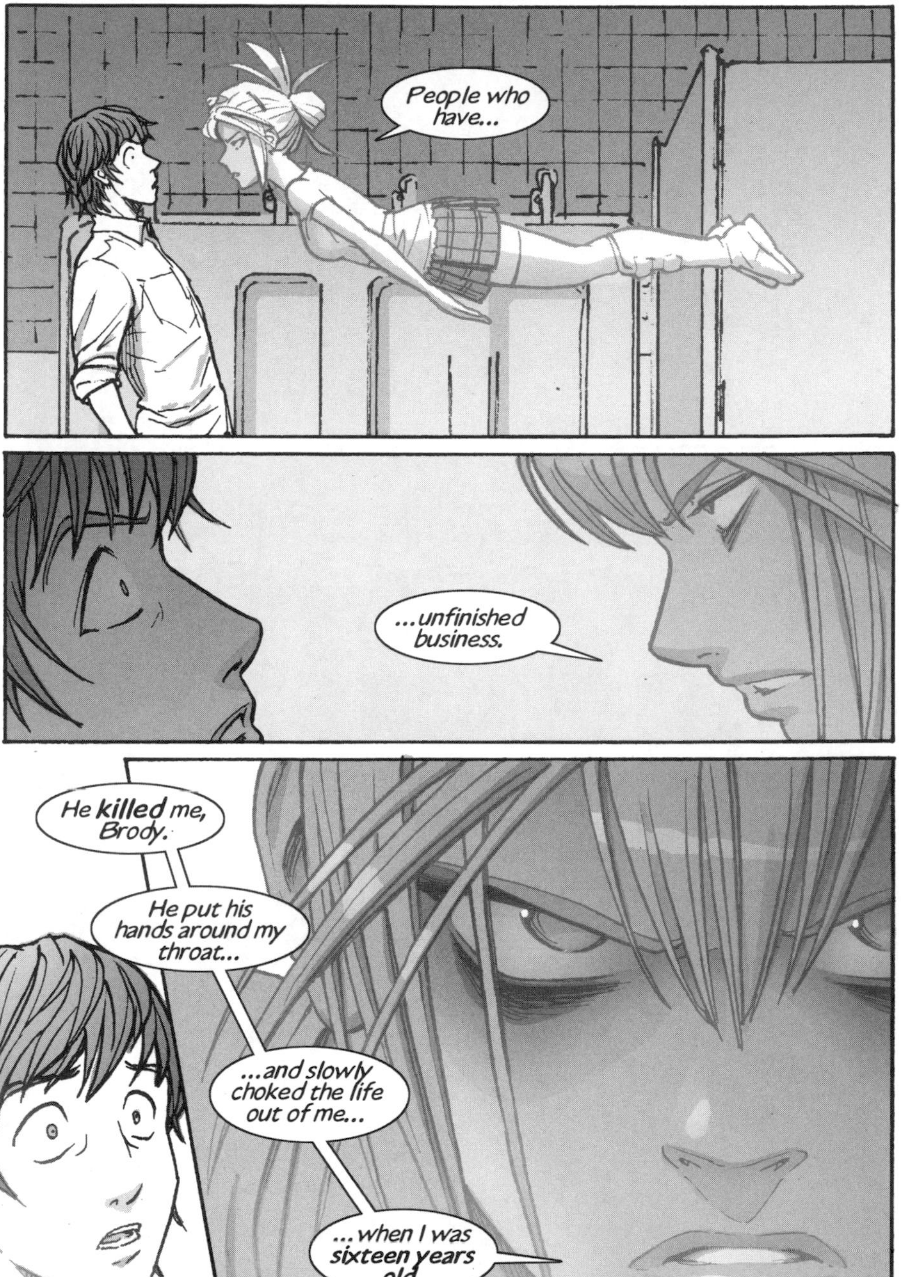
People who have...
...unfinished business.
He **killed** me, Brody.
He put his hands around my throat...
...and slowly choked the life out of me...
...when I was **sixteen years old.**

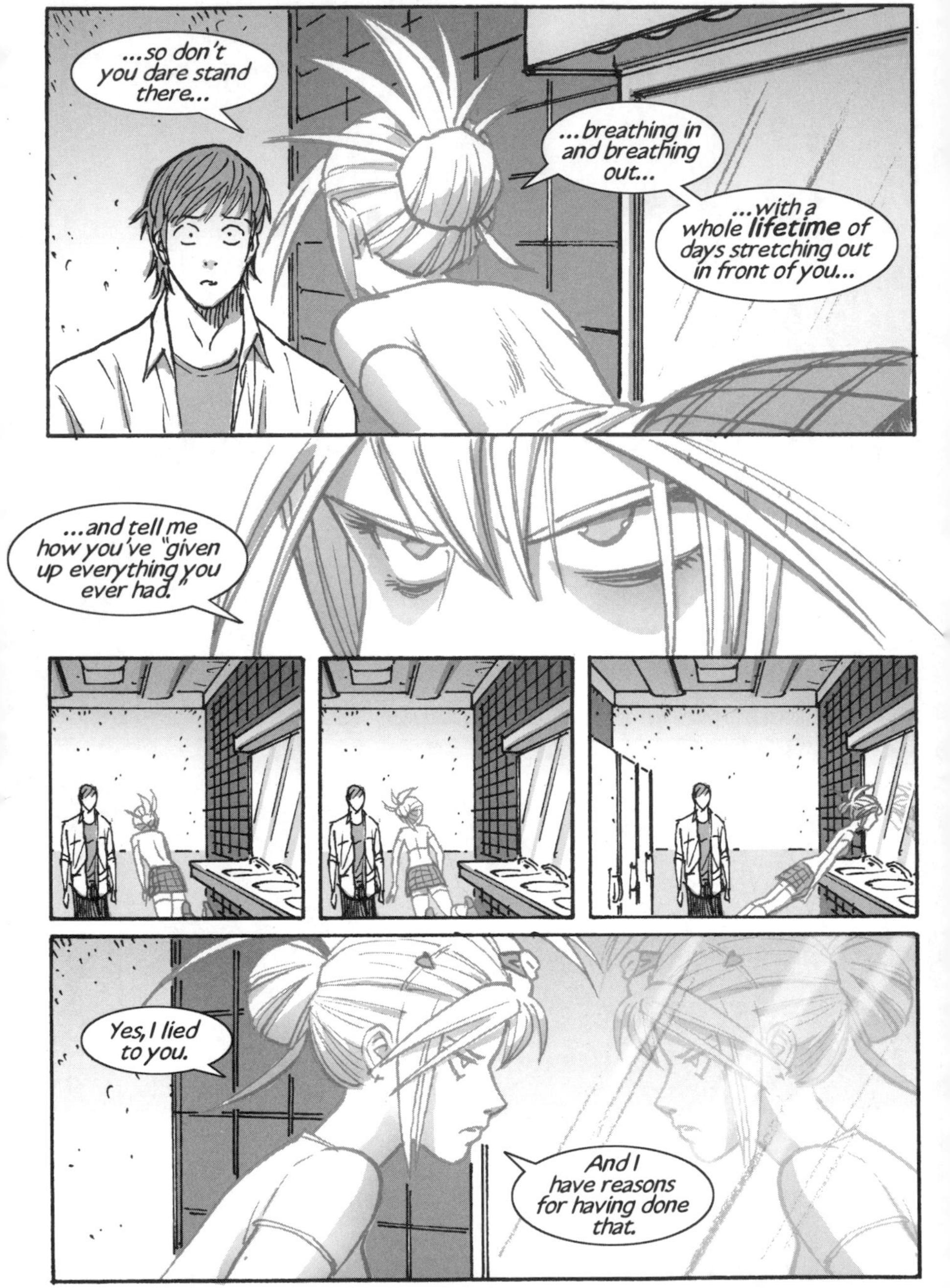
...so don't you dare stand there...
...breathing in and breathing out...
...with a whole **lifetime** of days stretching out in front of you...
...and tell me how you've "given up everything you ever had."
Yes, I lied to you.
And I have reasons for having done that.

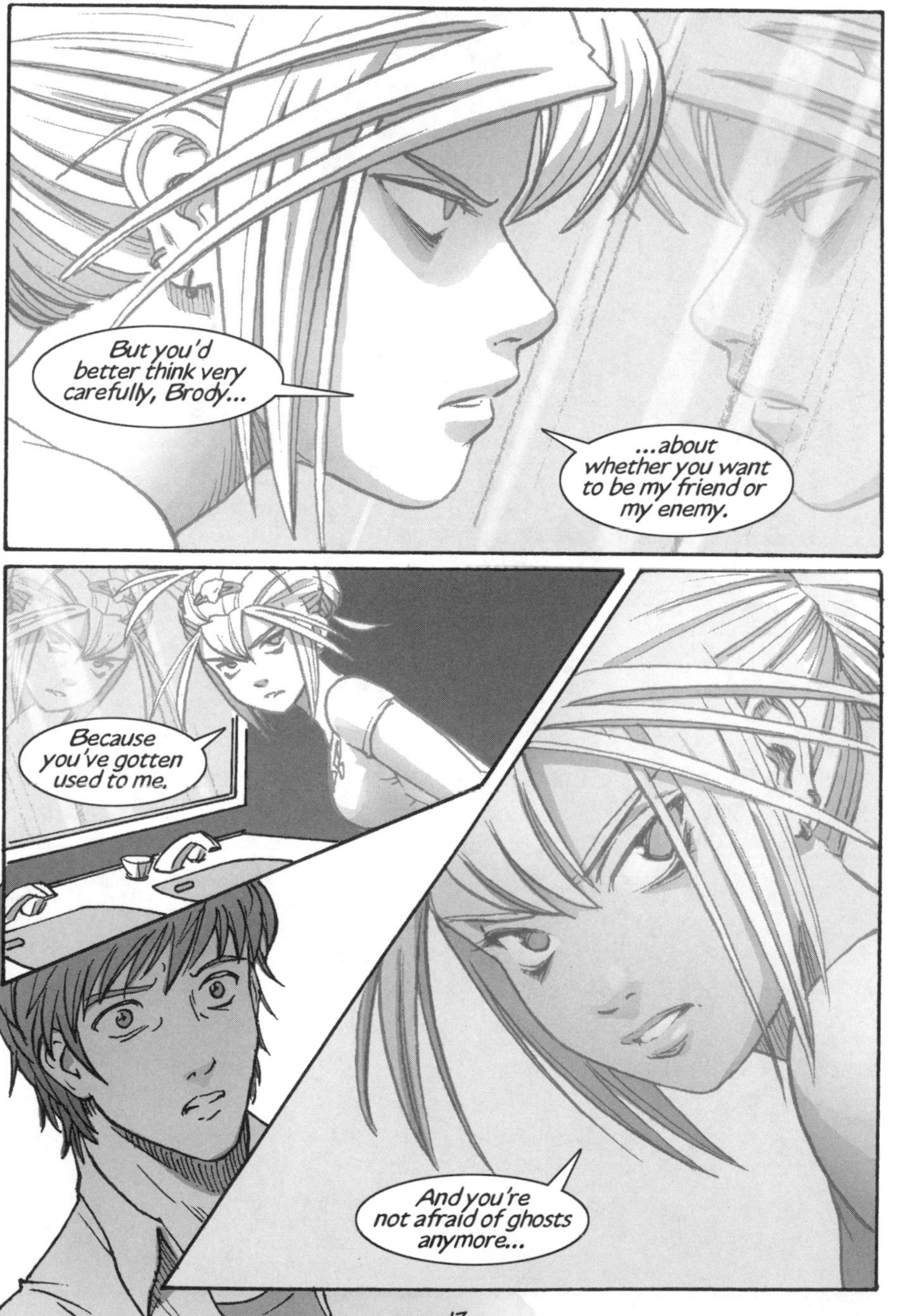
But you'd better think very carefully, Brody...
...about whether you want to be my friend or my enemy.
Because you've gotten used to me.
And you're not afraid of ghosts anymore...

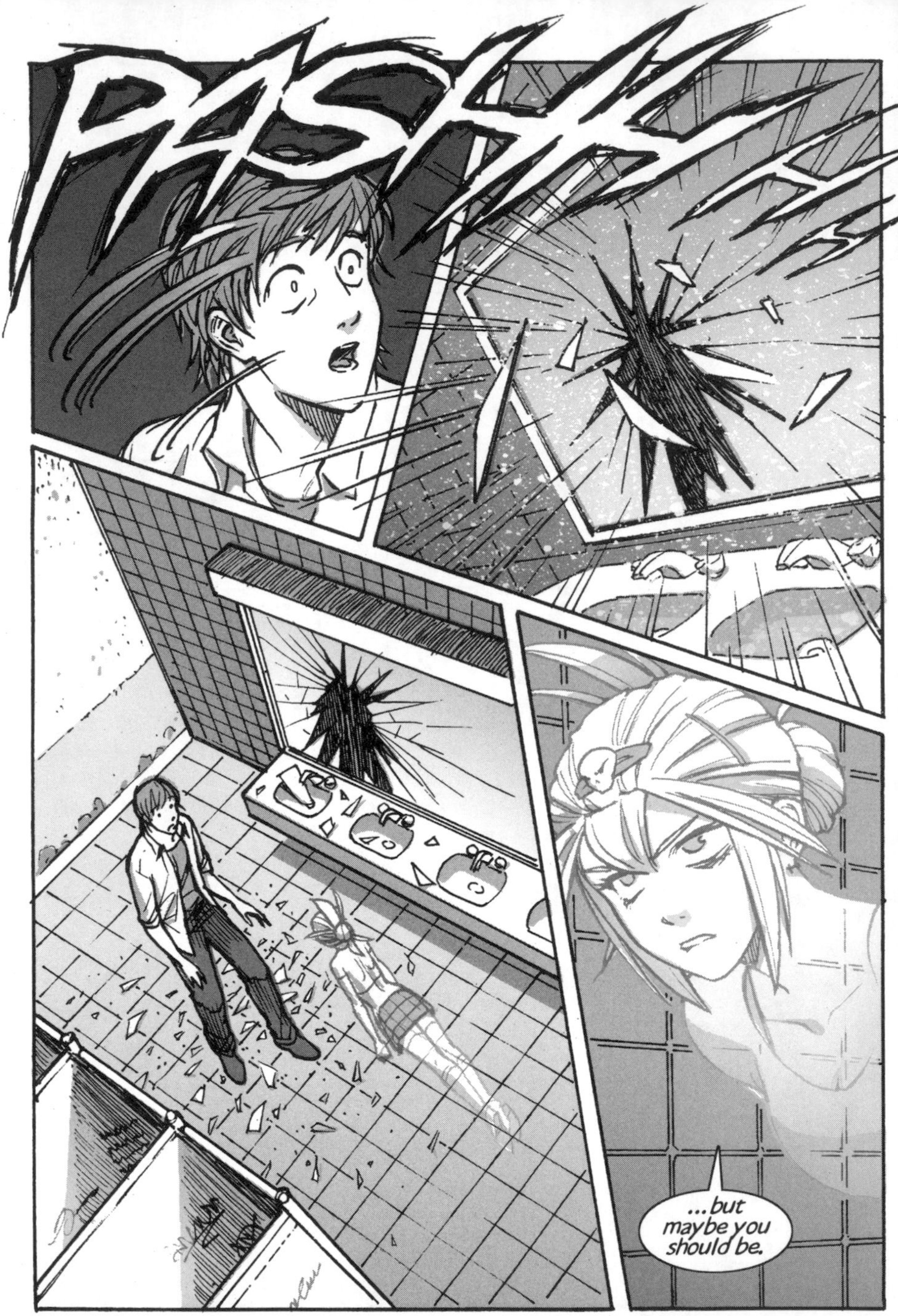
PASHAAASH
...but maybe you should be.

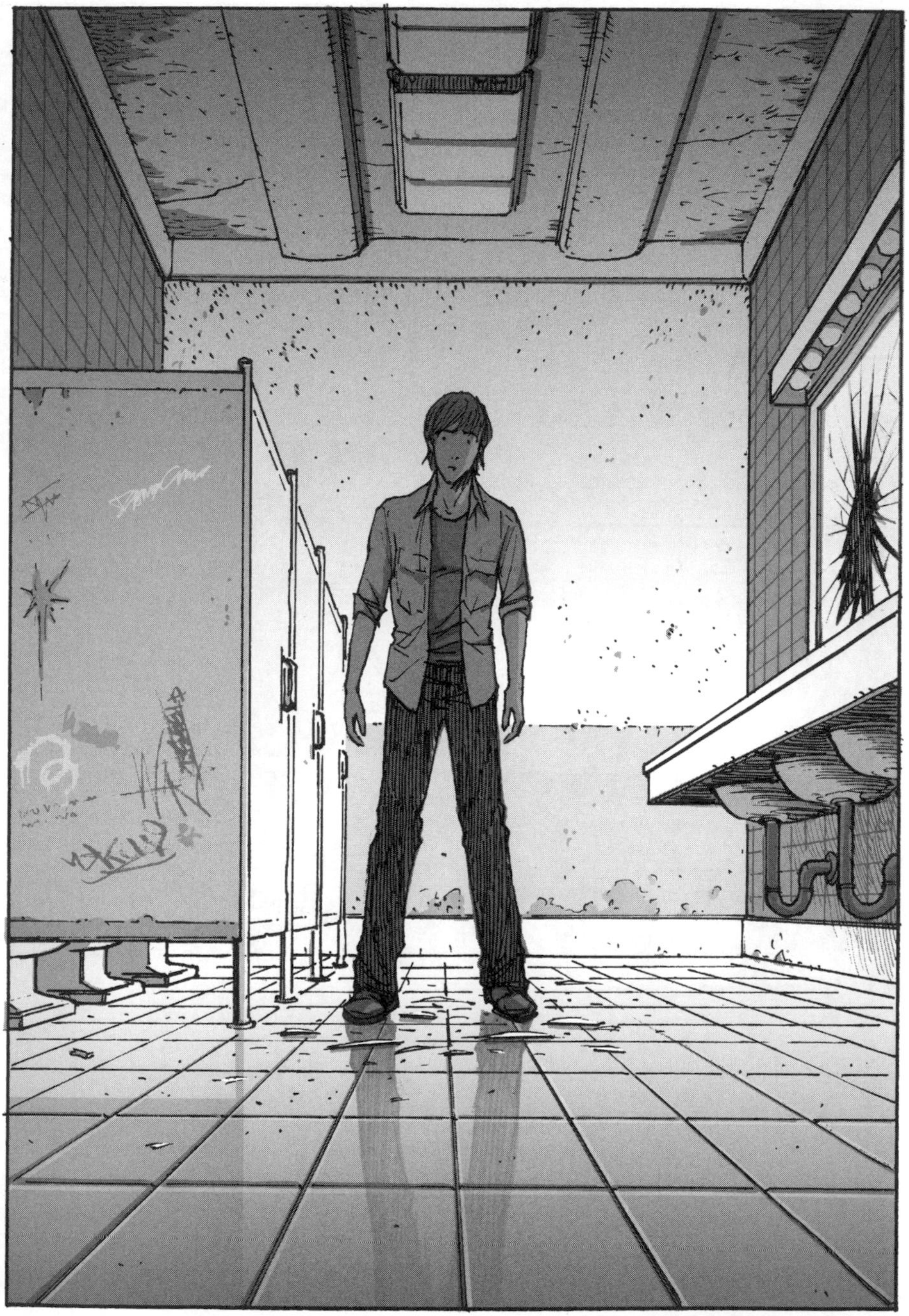

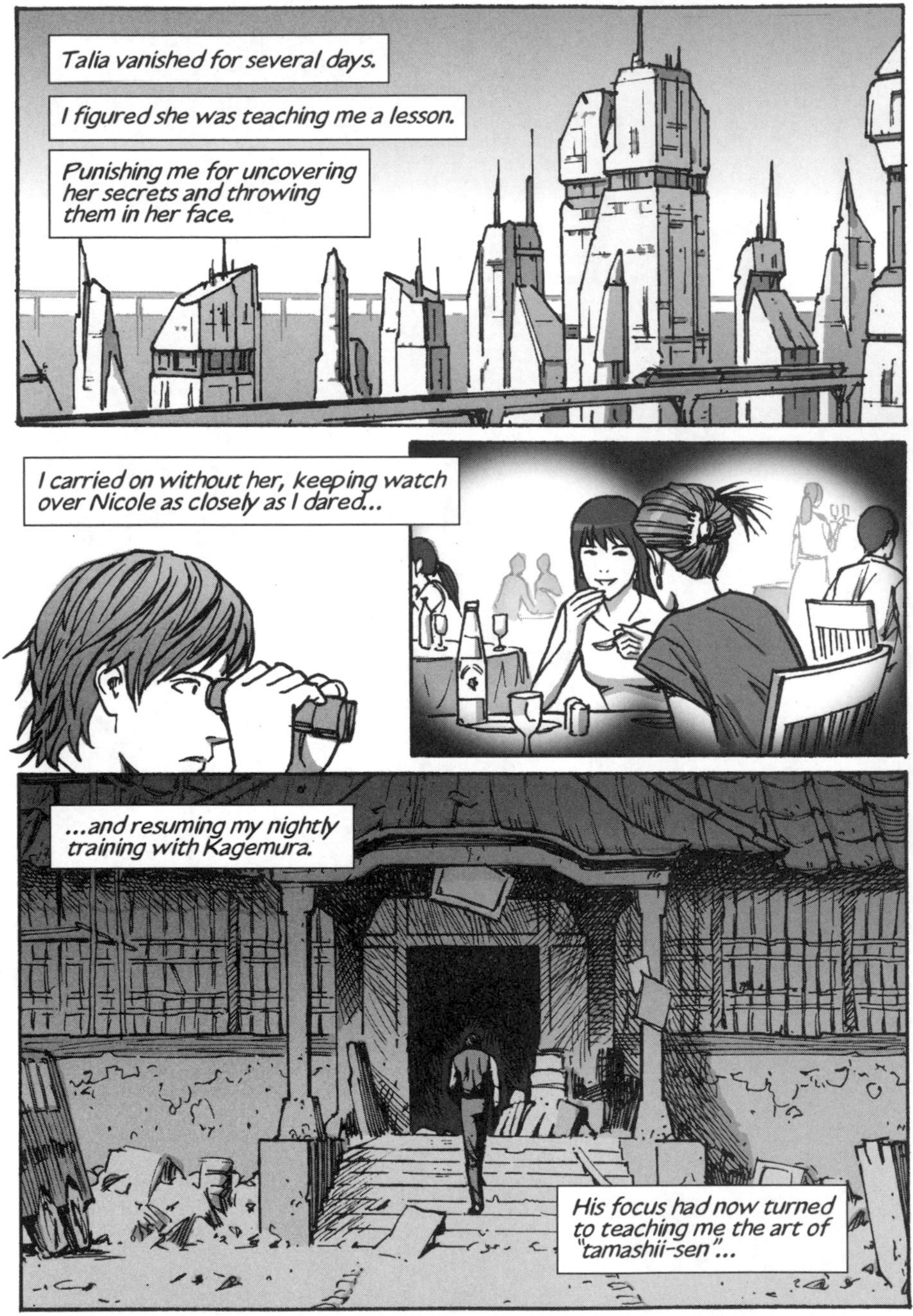
Talia vanished for several days.
I figured she was teaching me a lesson.
Punishing me for uncovering her secrets and throwing them in her face.
I carried on without her, keeping watch over Nicole as closely as I dared...
...and resuming my nightly training with Kagemura.
His focus had now turned to teaching me the art of "tamashii-sen"...

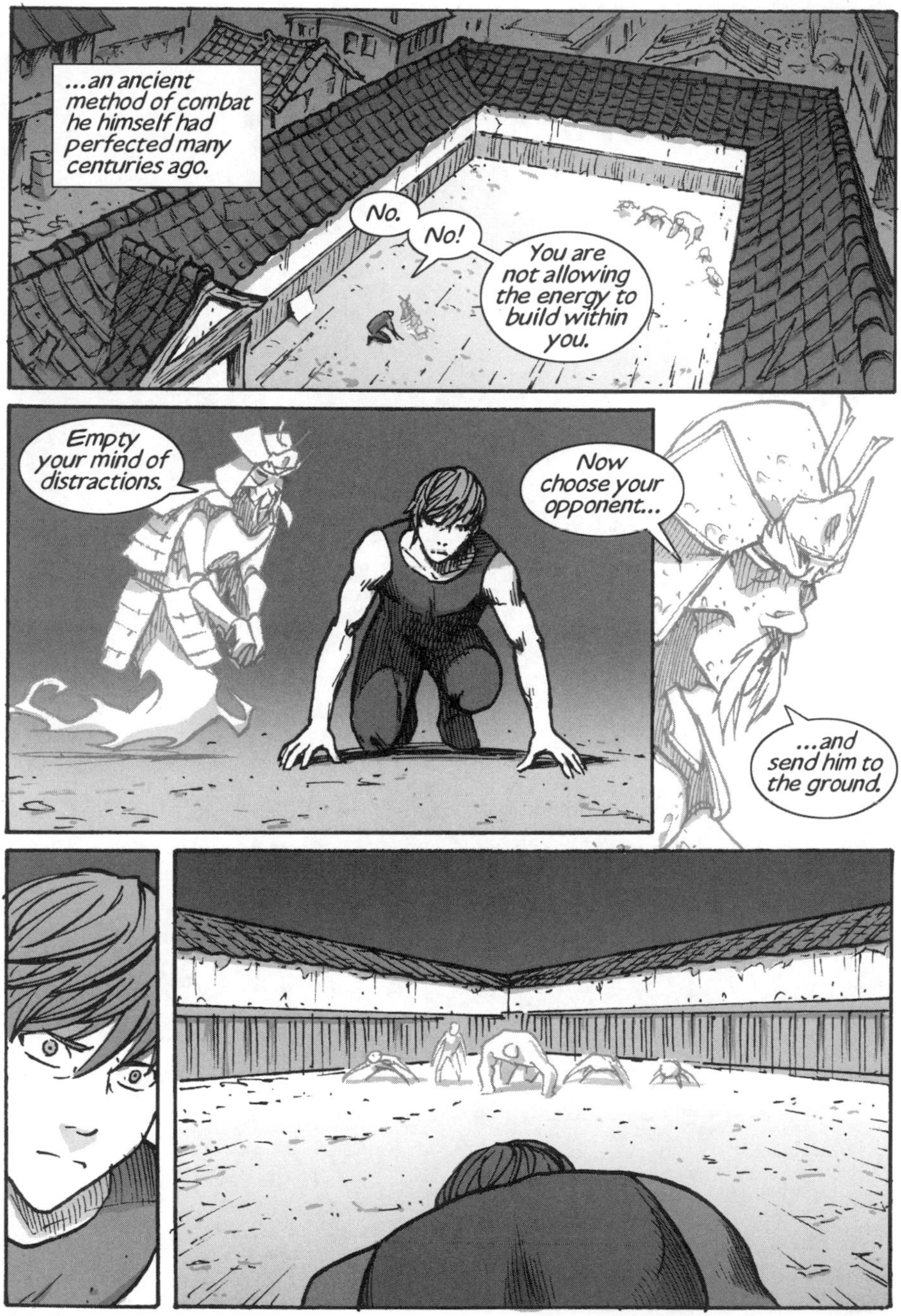
...an ancient method of combat he himself had perfected many centuries ago.
No.
No!
You are not allowing the energy to build within you.
Empty your mind of distractions.
Now choose your opponent...
...and send him to the ground.

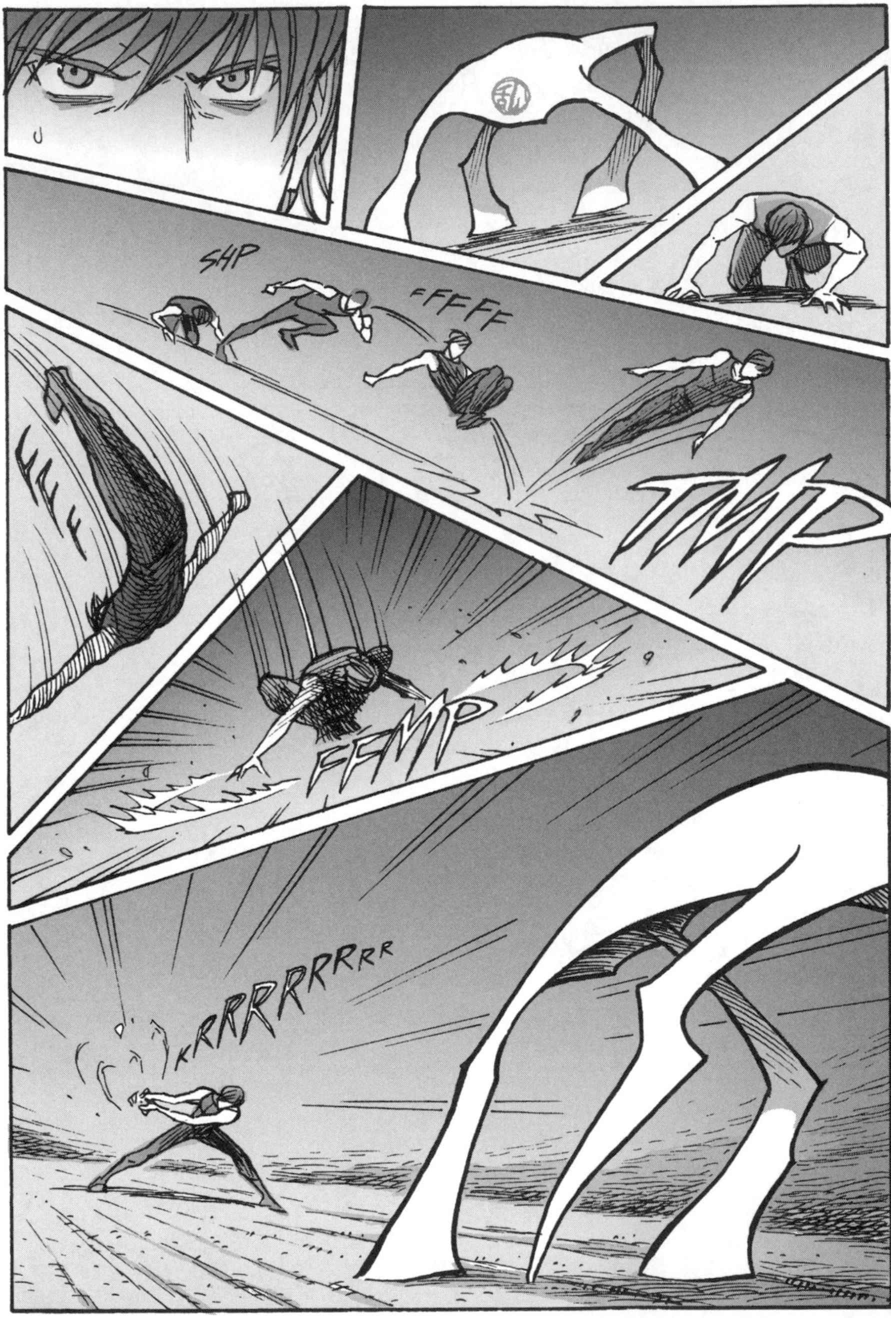

SHP
FFFFF
TMP
FFMP
KRRRRRRRR

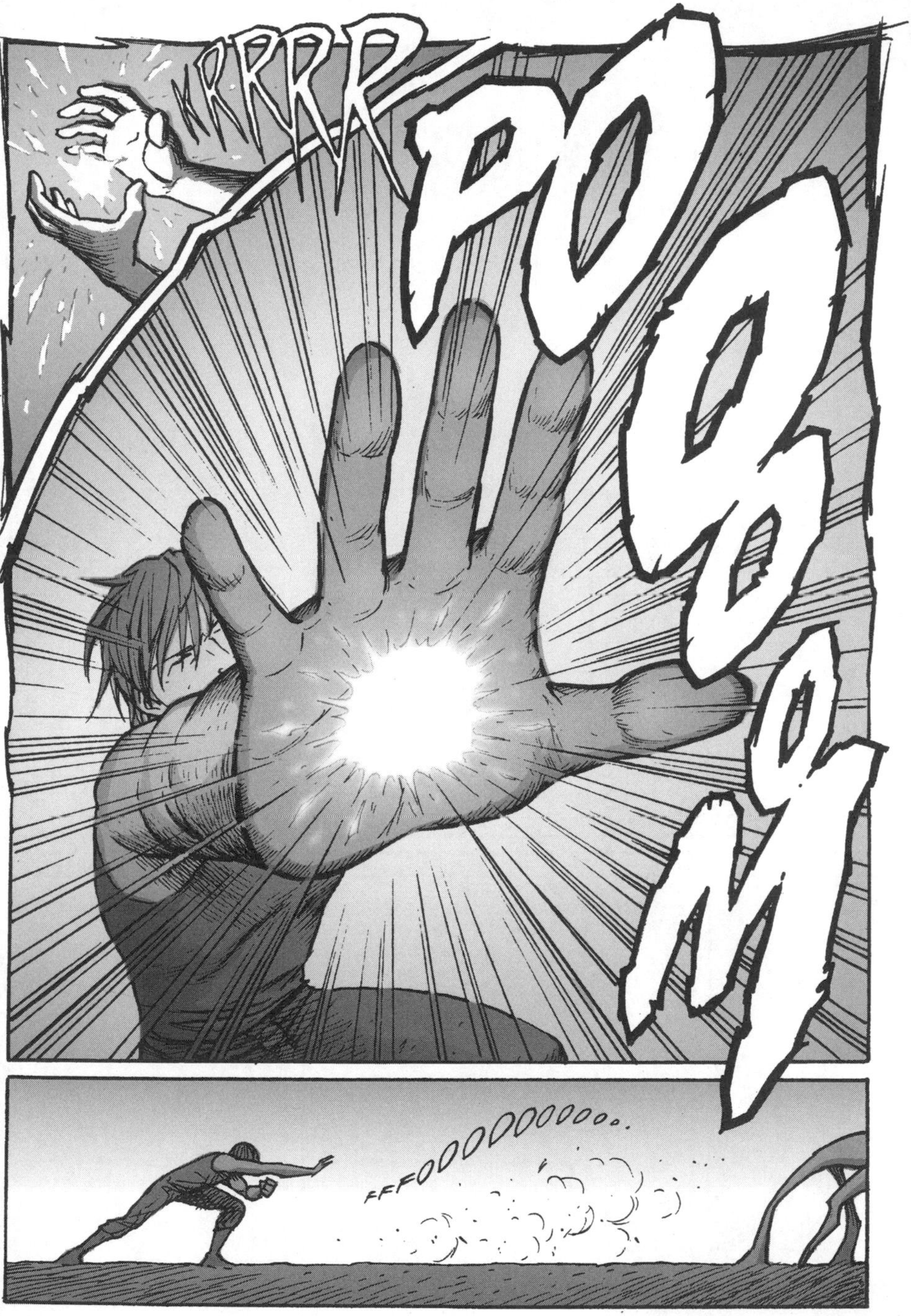
KRRRRR
POSSSH
FFFOOOOOOOOOOOoo..

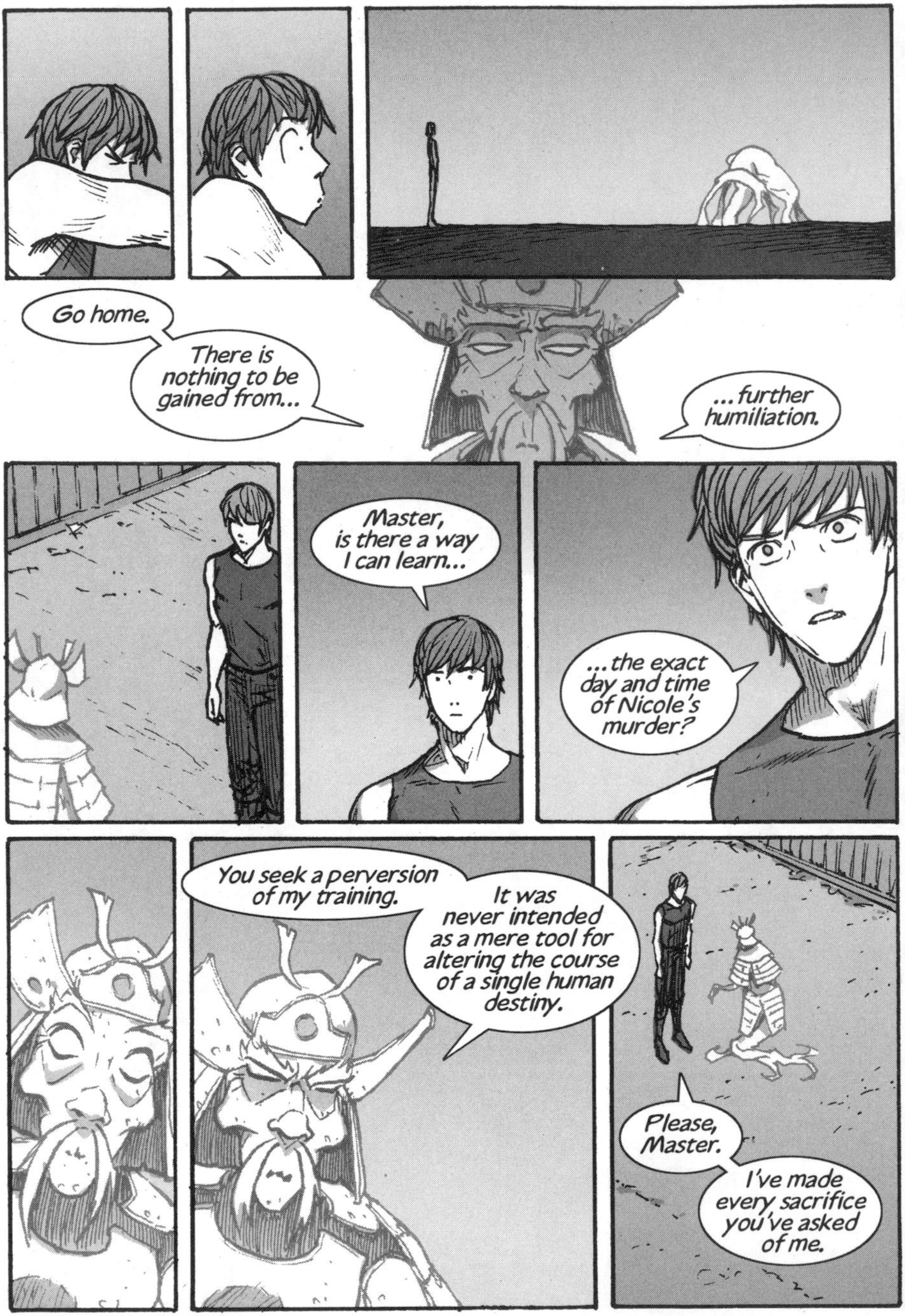
Go home.
There is nothing to be gained from...
...further humiliation.
Master, is there a way I can learn...
...the exact day and time of Nicole's murder?
You seek a perversion of my training.
It was never intended as a mere tool for altering the course of a single human destiny.
Please, Master.
I've made every sacrifice you've asked of me.

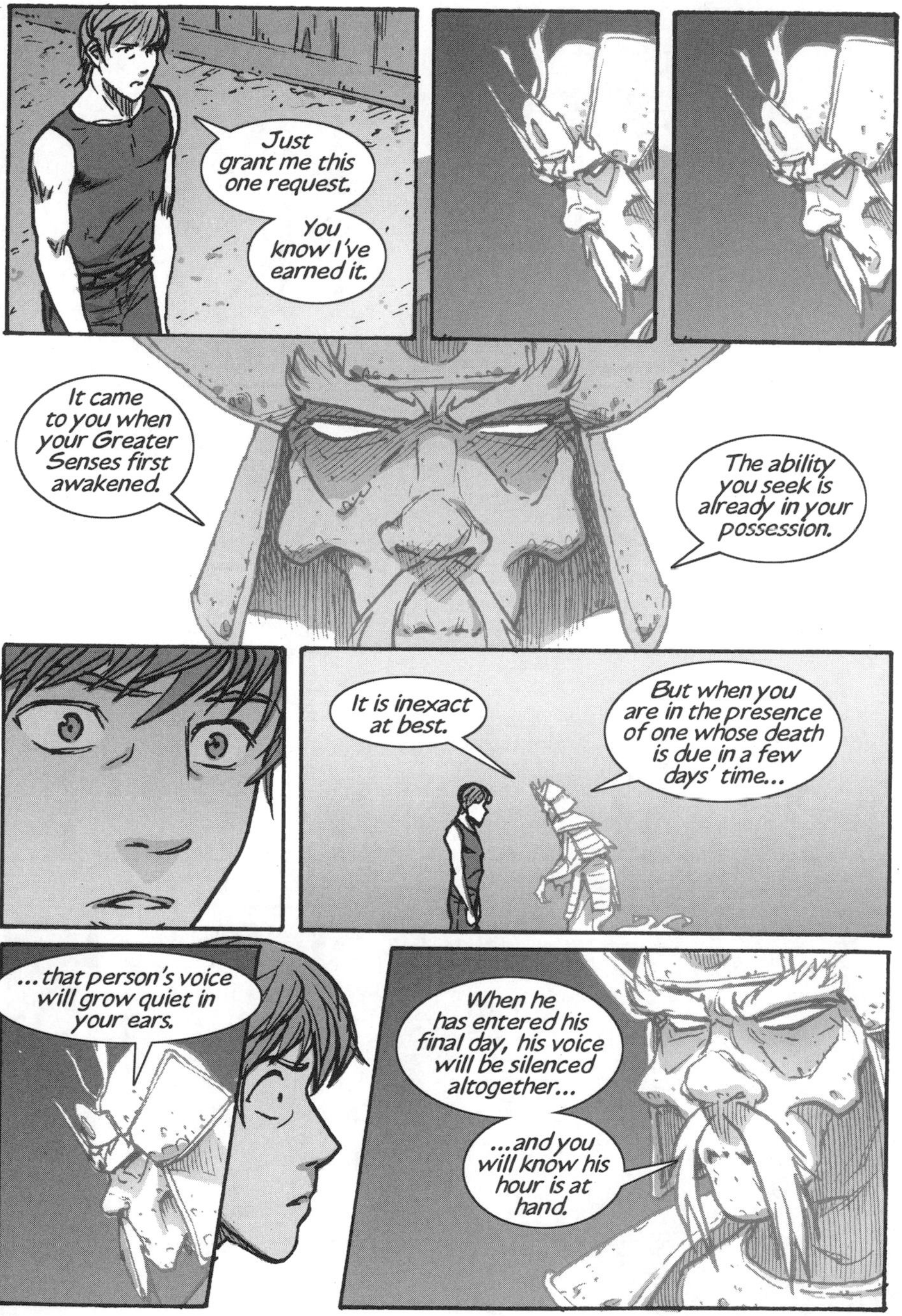
Just grant me this one request.
You know I've earned it.
The ability you seek is already in your possession.
It came to you when your Greater Senses first awakened.
It is inexact at best.
But when you are in the presence of one whose death is due in a few days' time...
...that person's voice will grow quiet in your ears.
When he has entered his final day, his voice will be silenced altogether...
...and you will know his hour is at hand.

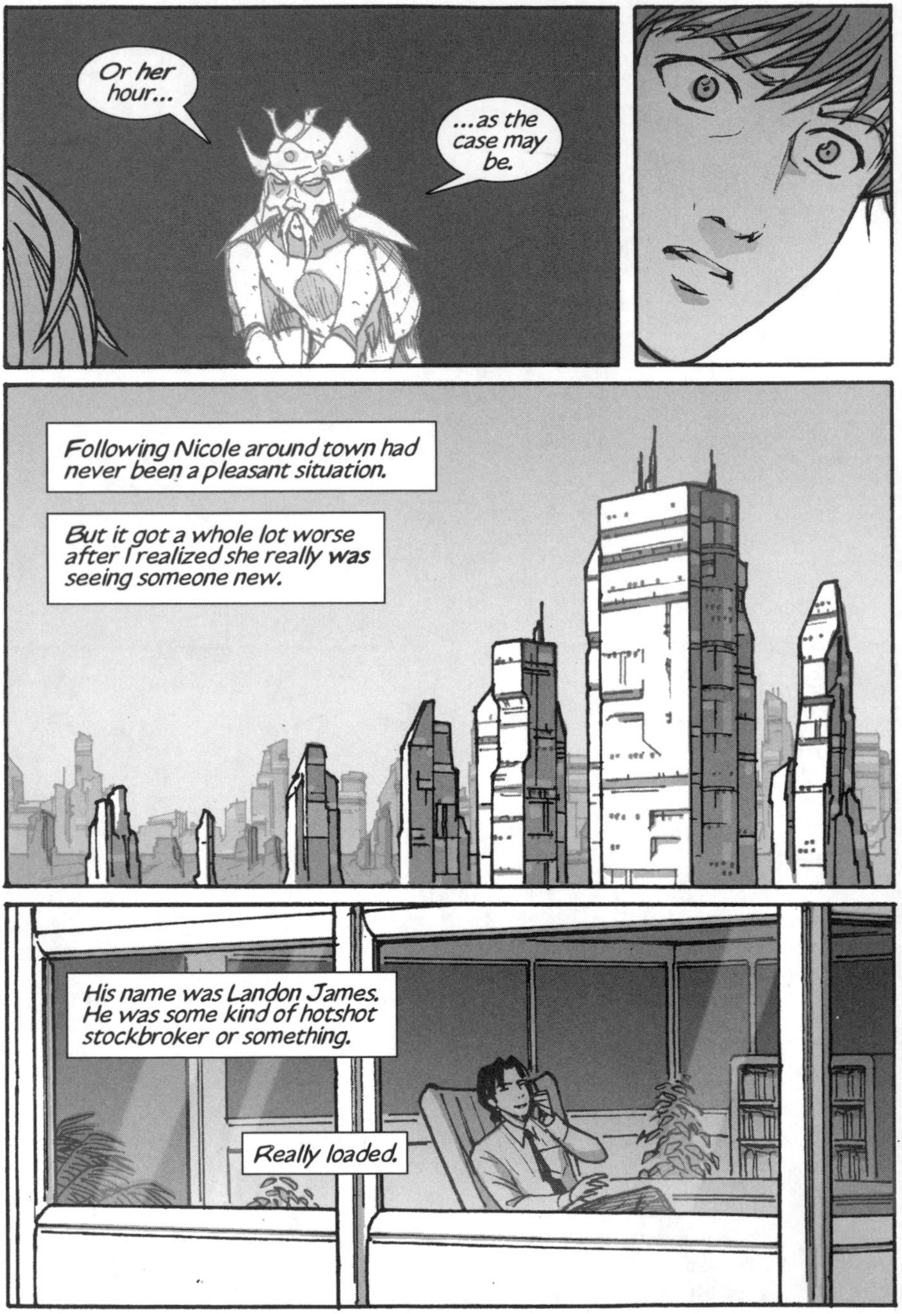
Or her hour...
...as the case may be.
Following Nicole around town had never been a pleasant situation.
But it got a whole lot worse after I realized she really **was** seeing someone new.
His name was Landon James. He was some kind of hotshot stockbroker or something.
Really loaded.

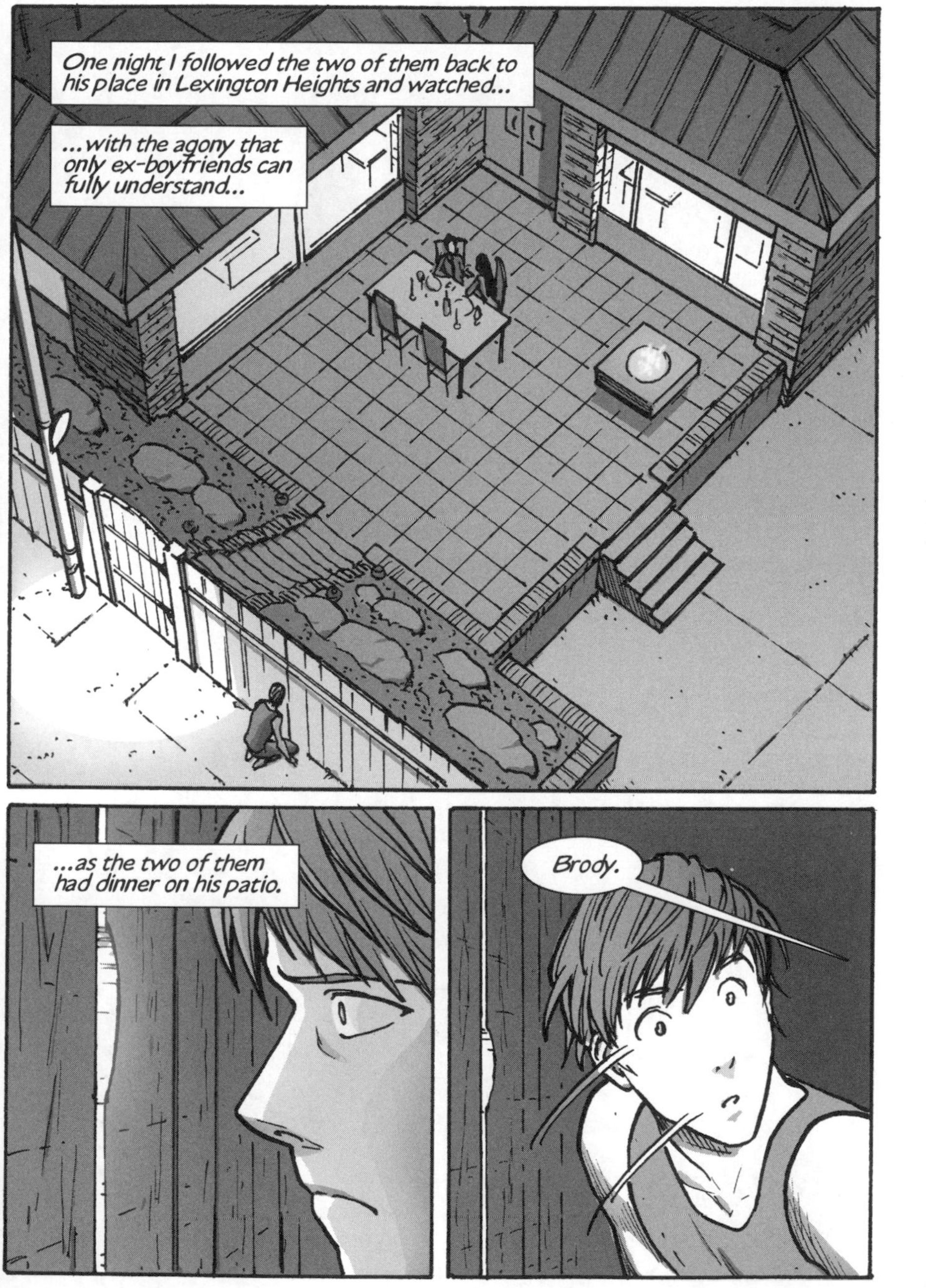
One night I followed the two of them back to his place in Lexington Heights and watched...
...with the agony that only ex-boyfriends can fully understand...
...as the two of them had dinner on his patio.
Brody.

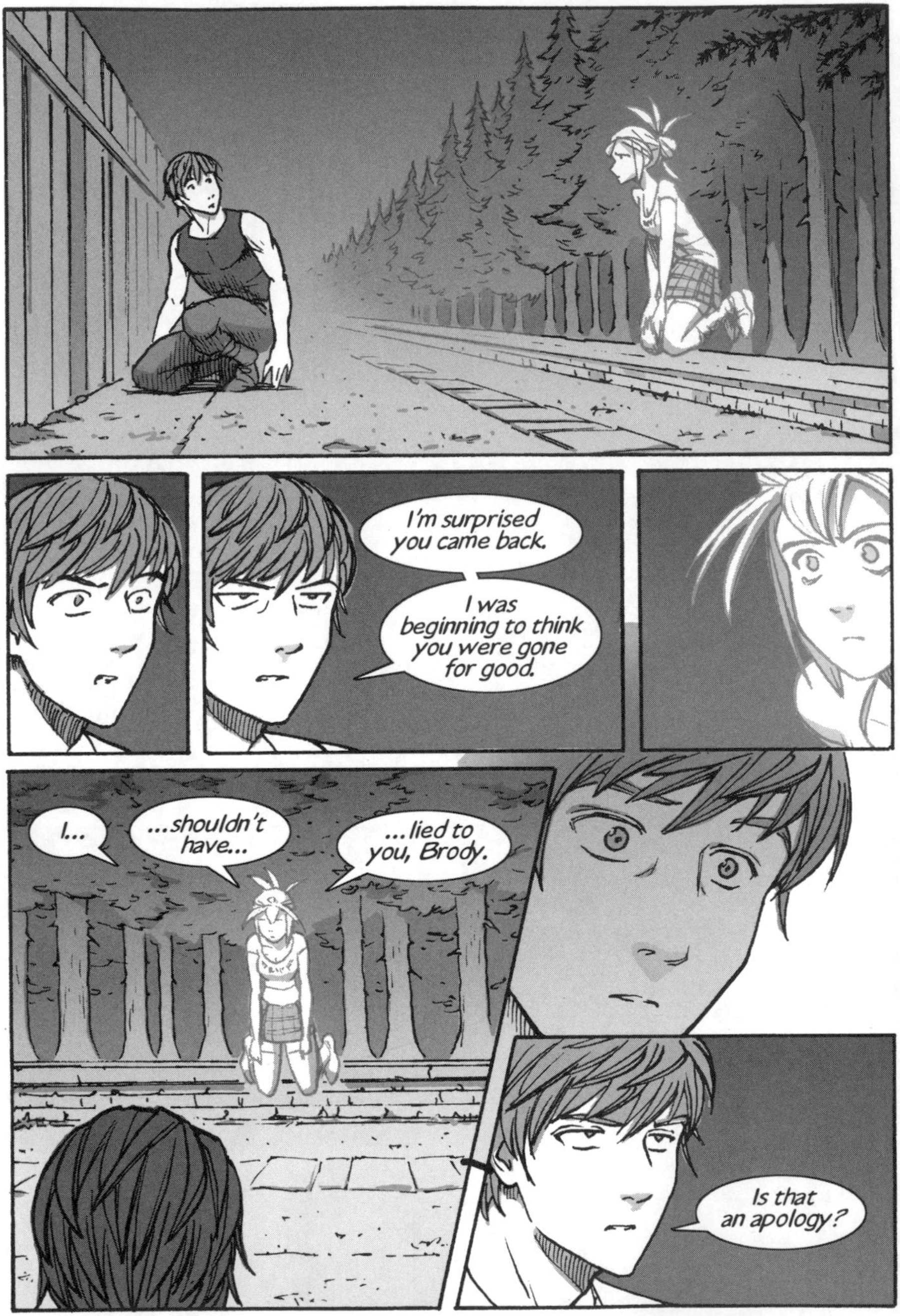
I'm surprised you came back.
I was beginning to think you were gone for good.
I...
...shouldn't have...
...lied to you, Brody.
Is that an apology?

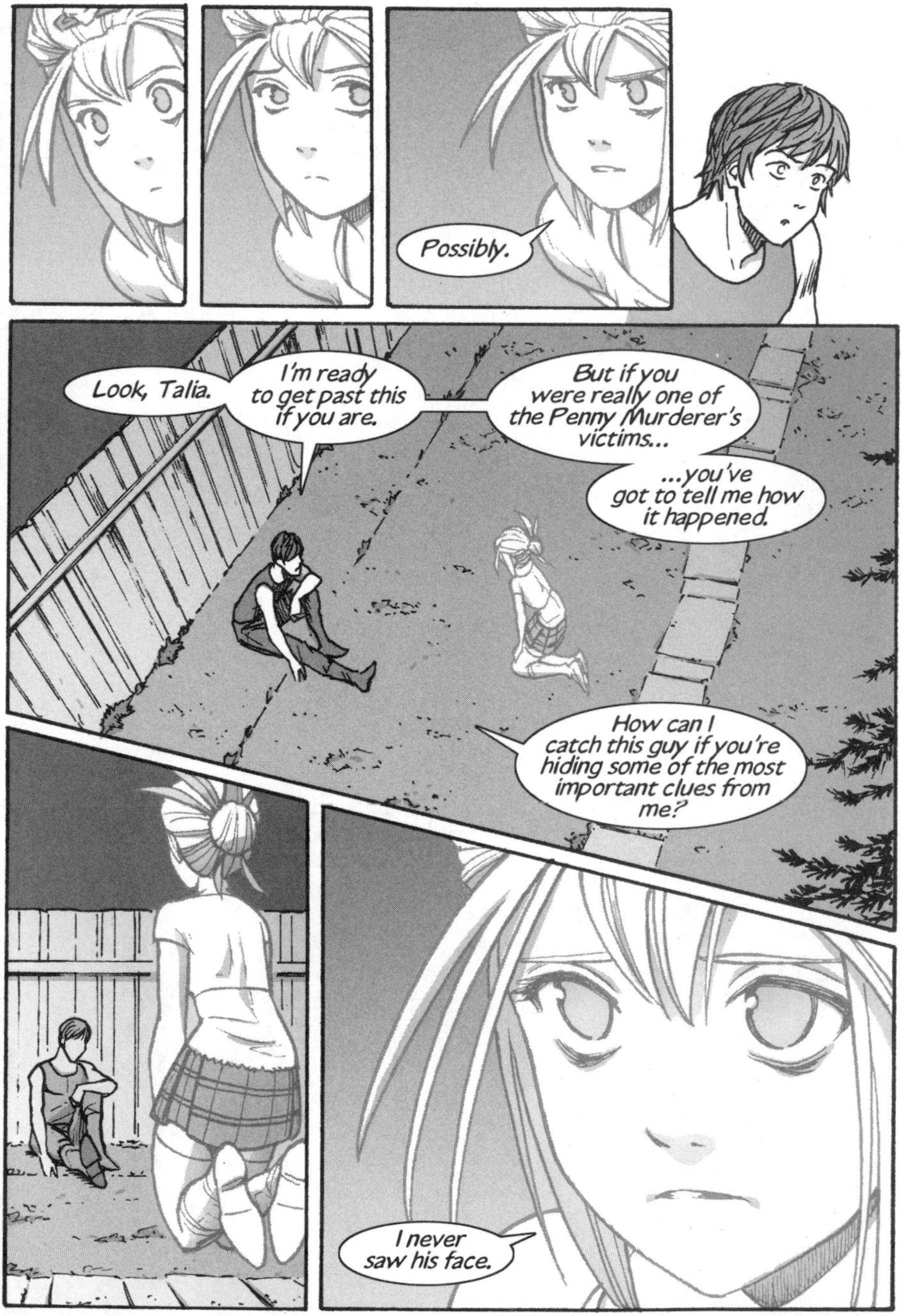
Possibly.
Look, Talia.
I'm ready to get past this if you are.
But if you were really one of the Penny Murderer's victims...
...you've got to tell me how it happened.
How can I catch this guy if you're hiding some of the most important clues from me?
I never saw his face.

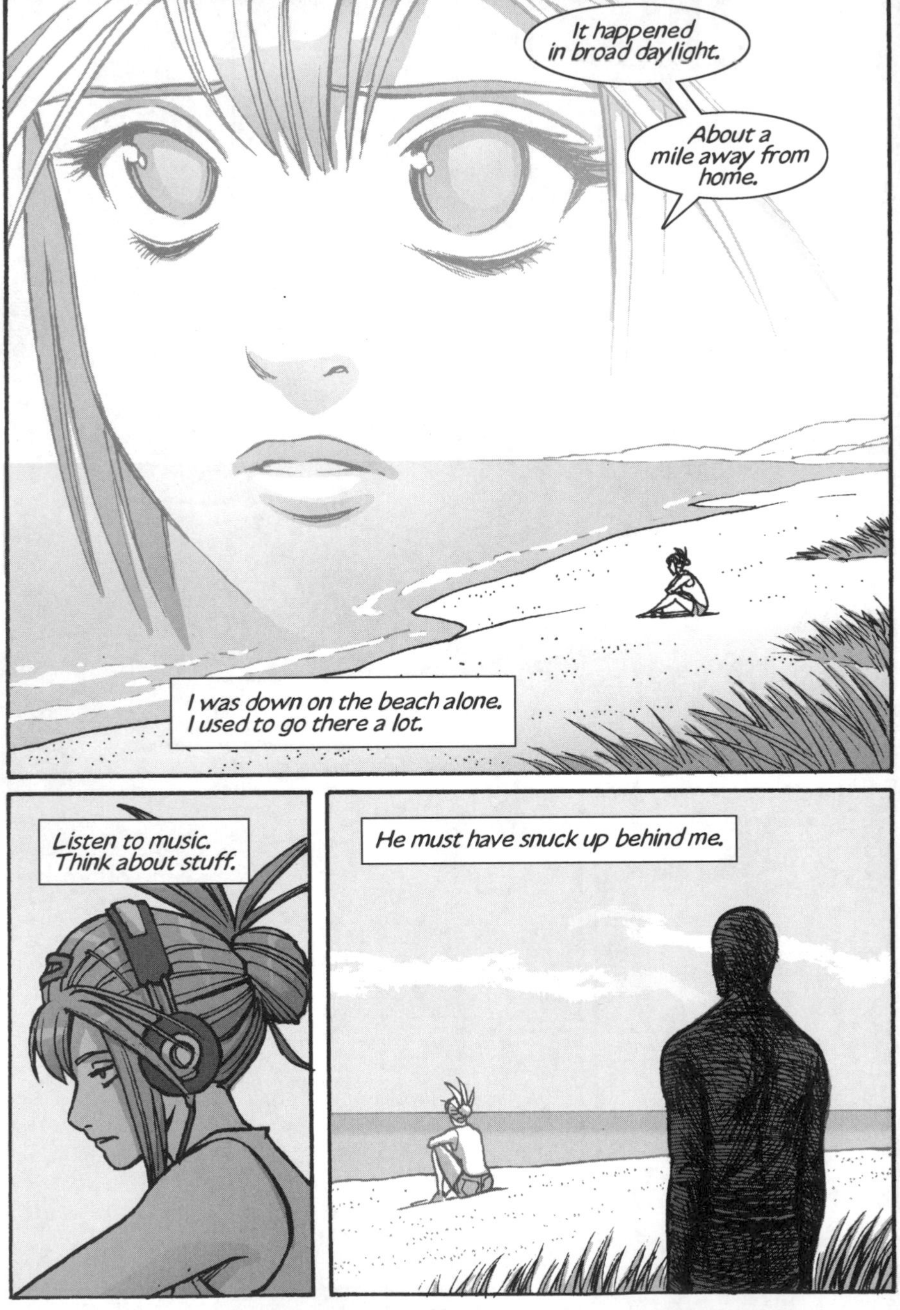
It happened in broad daylight.
About a mile away from home.
I was down on the beach alone. I used to go there a lot.
Listen to music. Think about stuff.
He must have snuck up behind me.

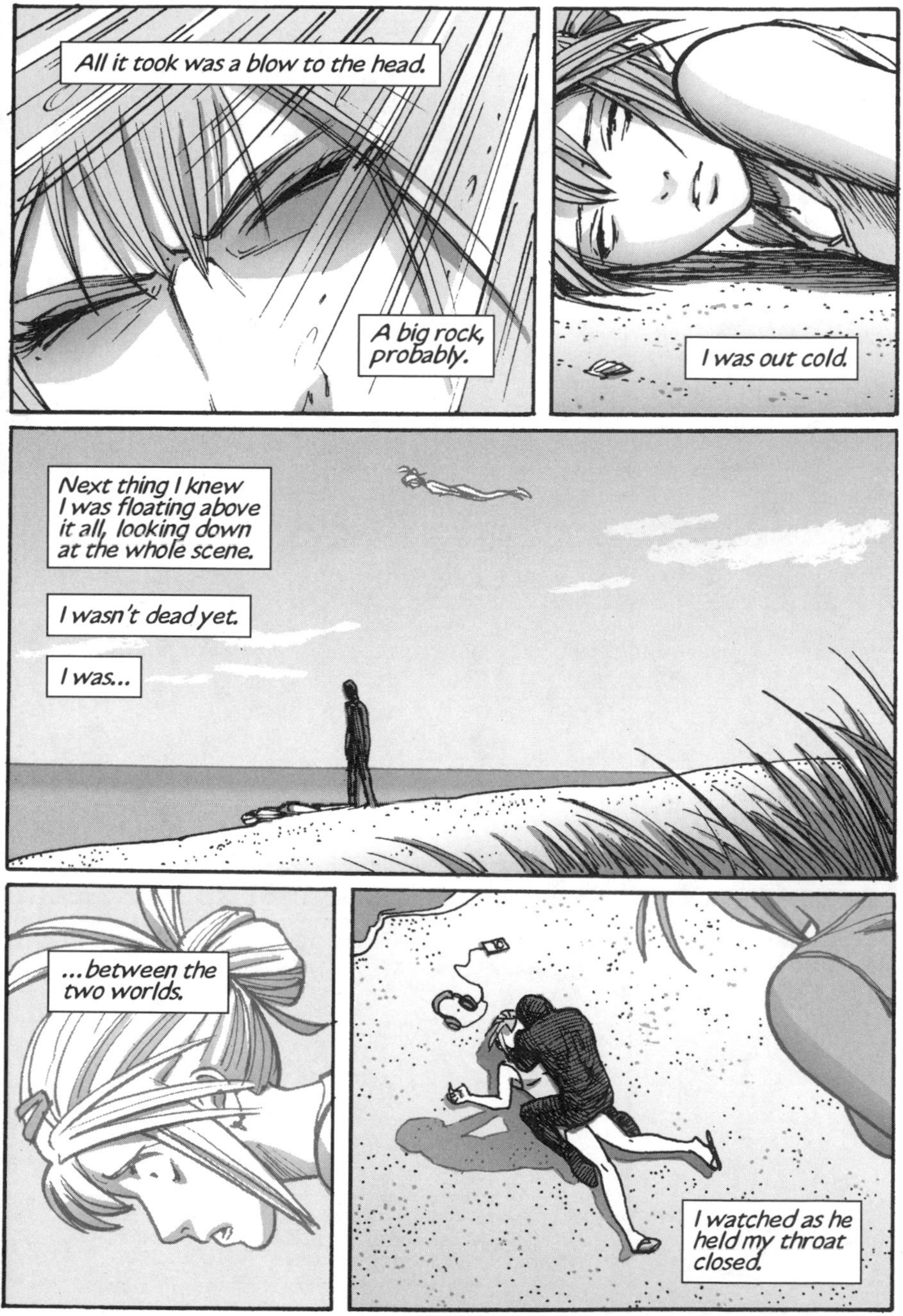
All it took was a blow to the head.
A big rock, probably.
I was out cold.
Next thing I knew I was floating above it all, looking down at the whole scene.
I wasn't dead yet.
I was...
...between the two worlds.
I watched as he held my throat closed.

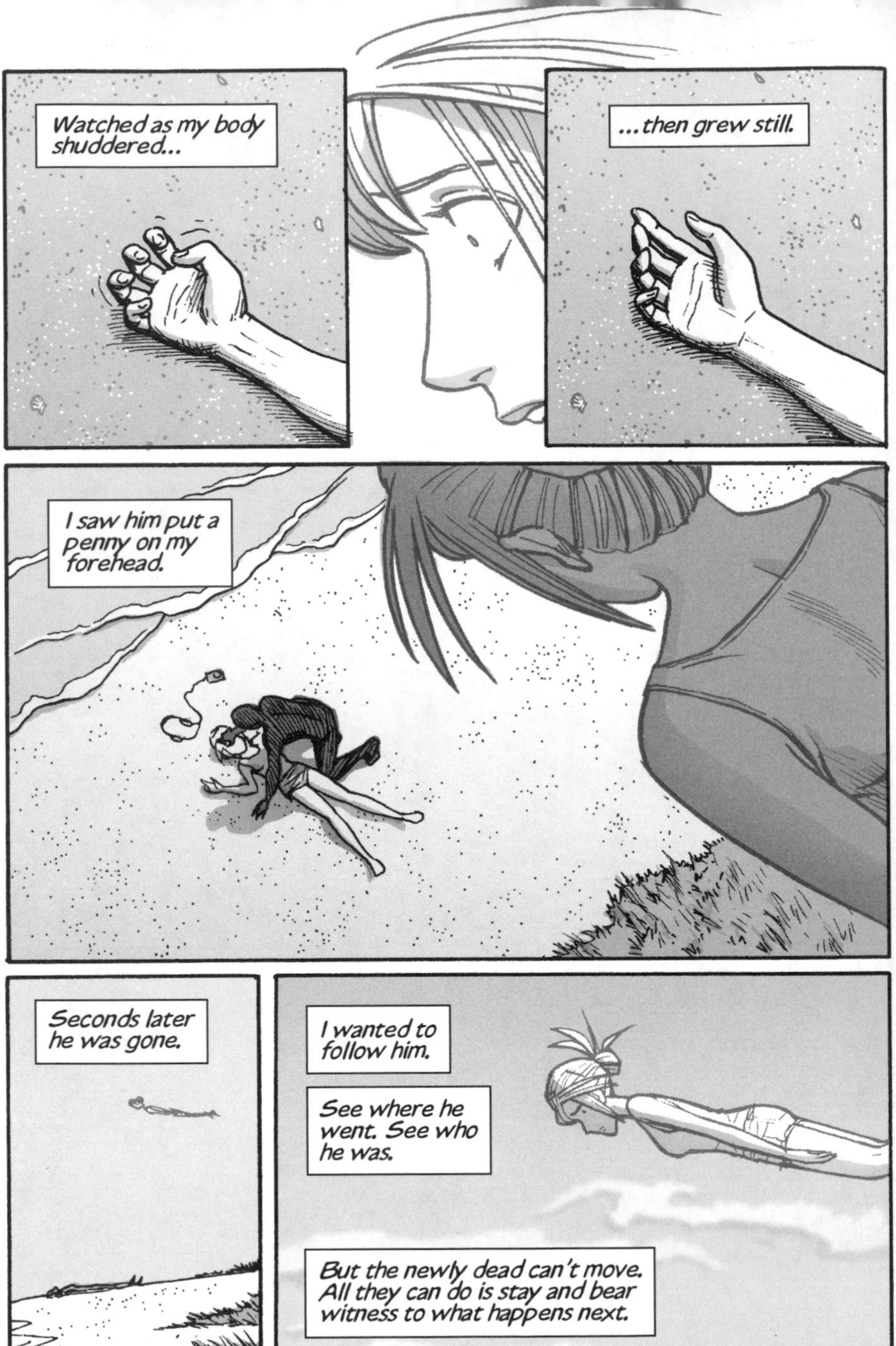

Watched as my body shuddered...
...then grew still.
I saw him put a penny on my forehead.
Seconds later he was gone.
I wanted to follow him.
See where he went. See who he was.
But the newly dead can't move. All they can do is stay and bear witness to what happens next.

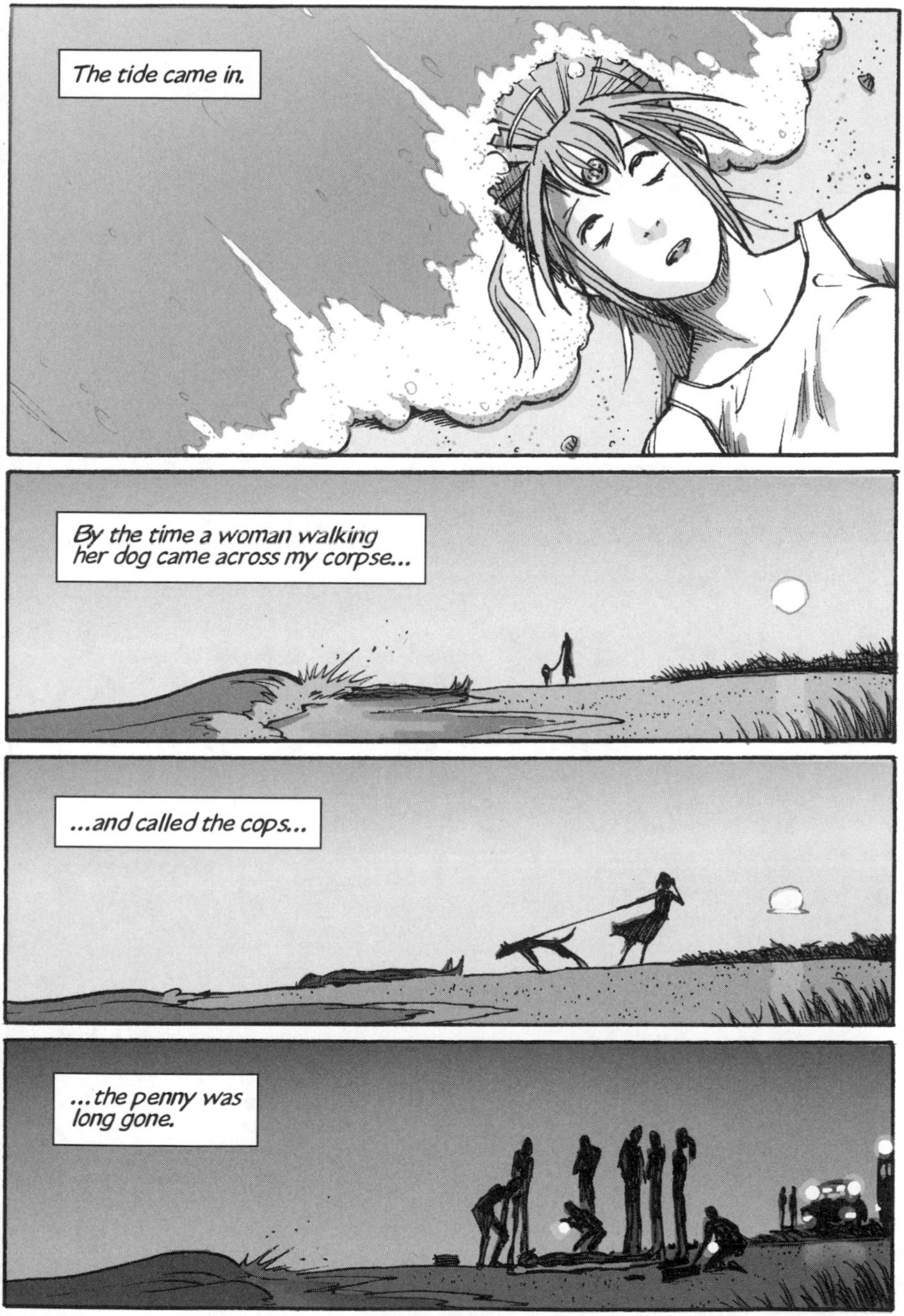
The tide came in.
By the time a woman walking her dog came across my corpse...
...and called the cops...
...the penny was long gone.

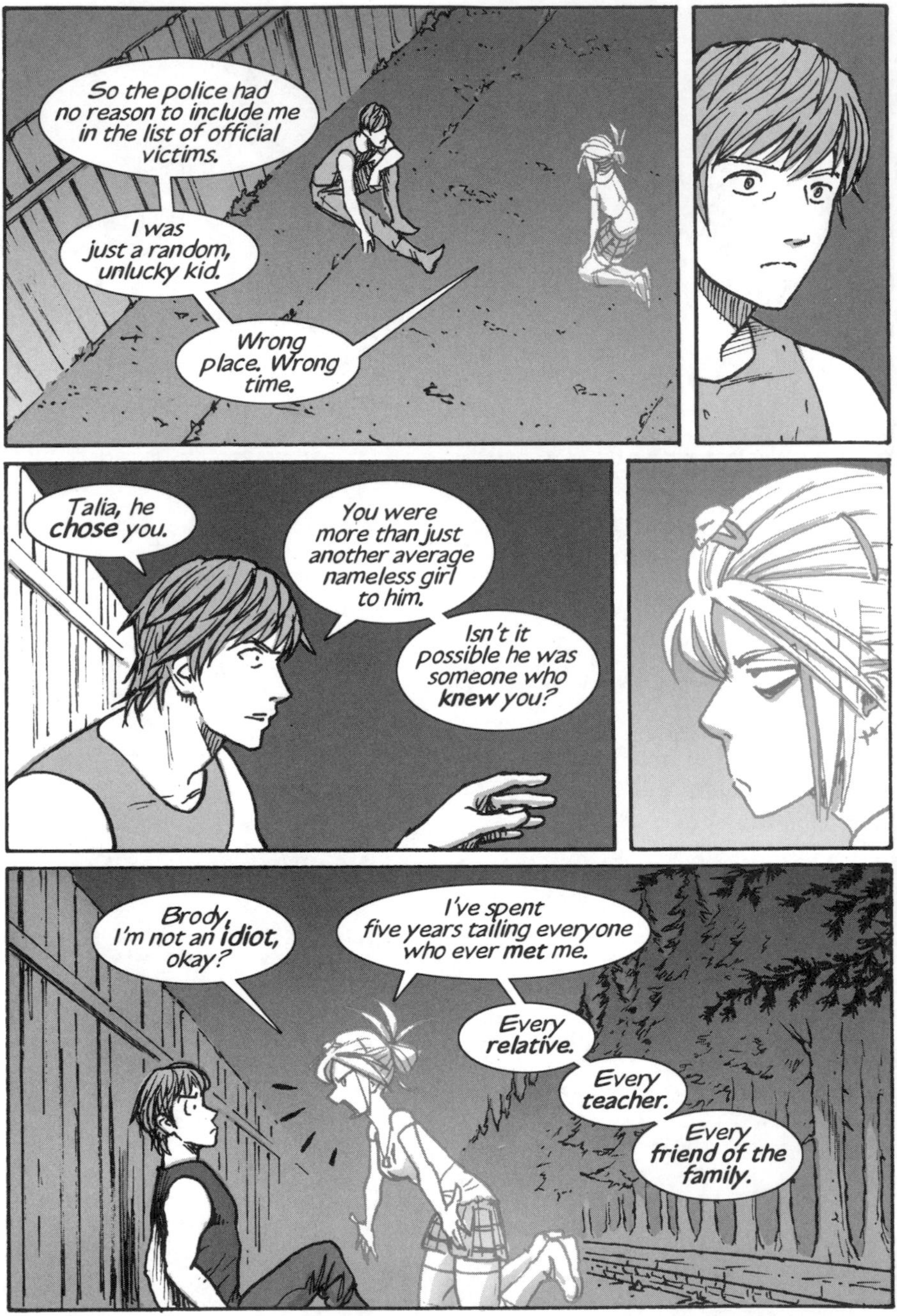
So the police had no reason to include me in the list of official victims.
I was just a random, unlucky kid.
Wrong place. Wrong time.
Talia, he **chose** you.
You were more than just another average nameless girl to him.
Isn't it possible he was someone who **knew** you?
Brody, I'm not an **idiot**, okay?
I've spent five years tailing everyone who ever **met** me.
Every **relative.**
Every **teacher.**
Every **friend of the family.**

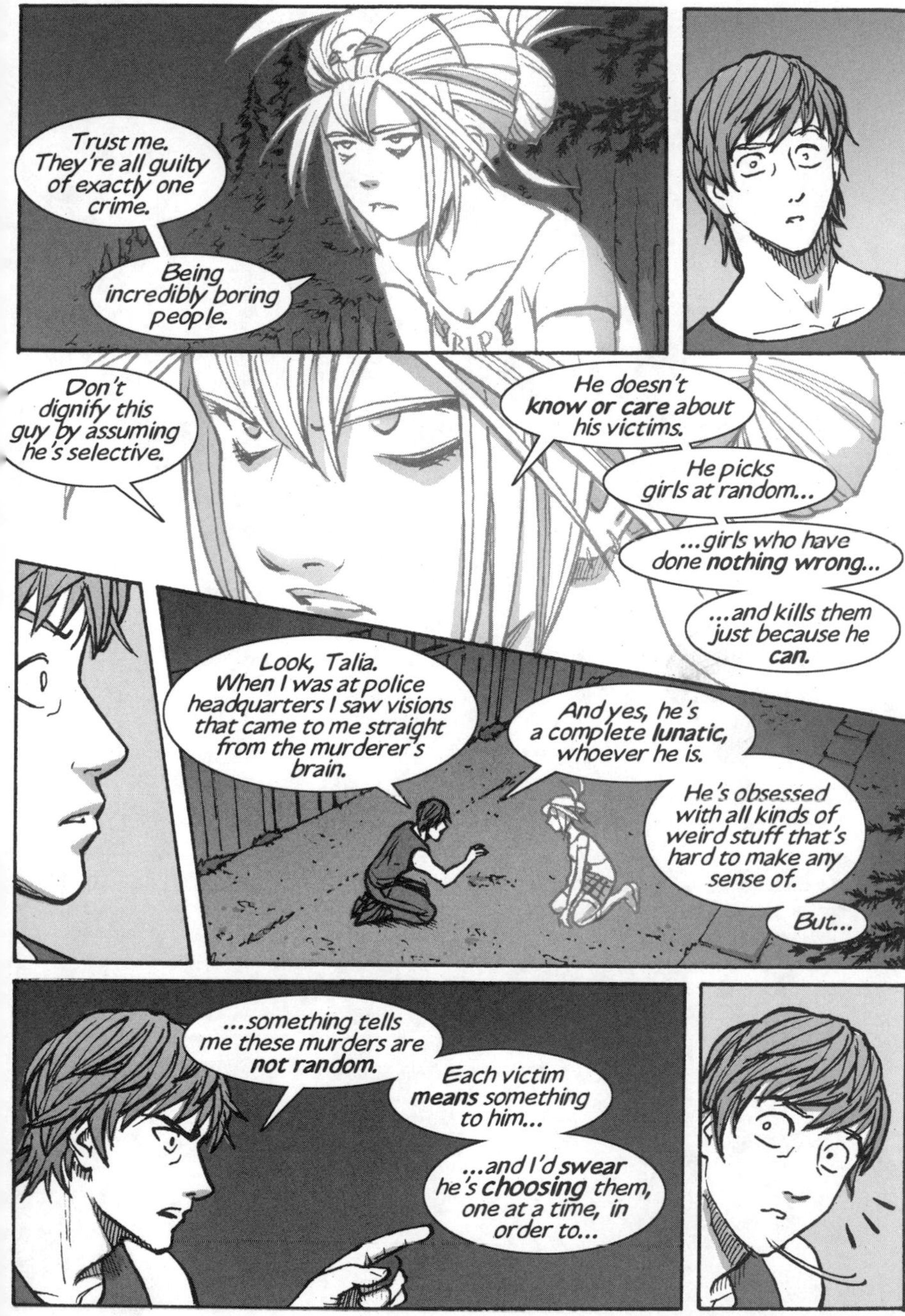
Trust me. They're all guilty of exactly one crime.
Being incredibly boring people.
RIP
Don't dignify this guy by assuming he's selective.
He doesn't **know or care** about his victims.
He picks girls at random...
...girls who have done **nothing wrong**...
...and kills them just because he **can.**
Look, Talia. When I was at police headquarters I saw visions that came to me straight from the murderer's brain.
And yes, he's a complete **lunatic,** whoever he is.
He's obsessed with all kinds of weird stuff that's hard to make any sense of.
But...
...something tells me these murders are **not random.**
Each victim **means** something to him...
...and I'd **swear** he's **choosing** them, one at a time, in order to...

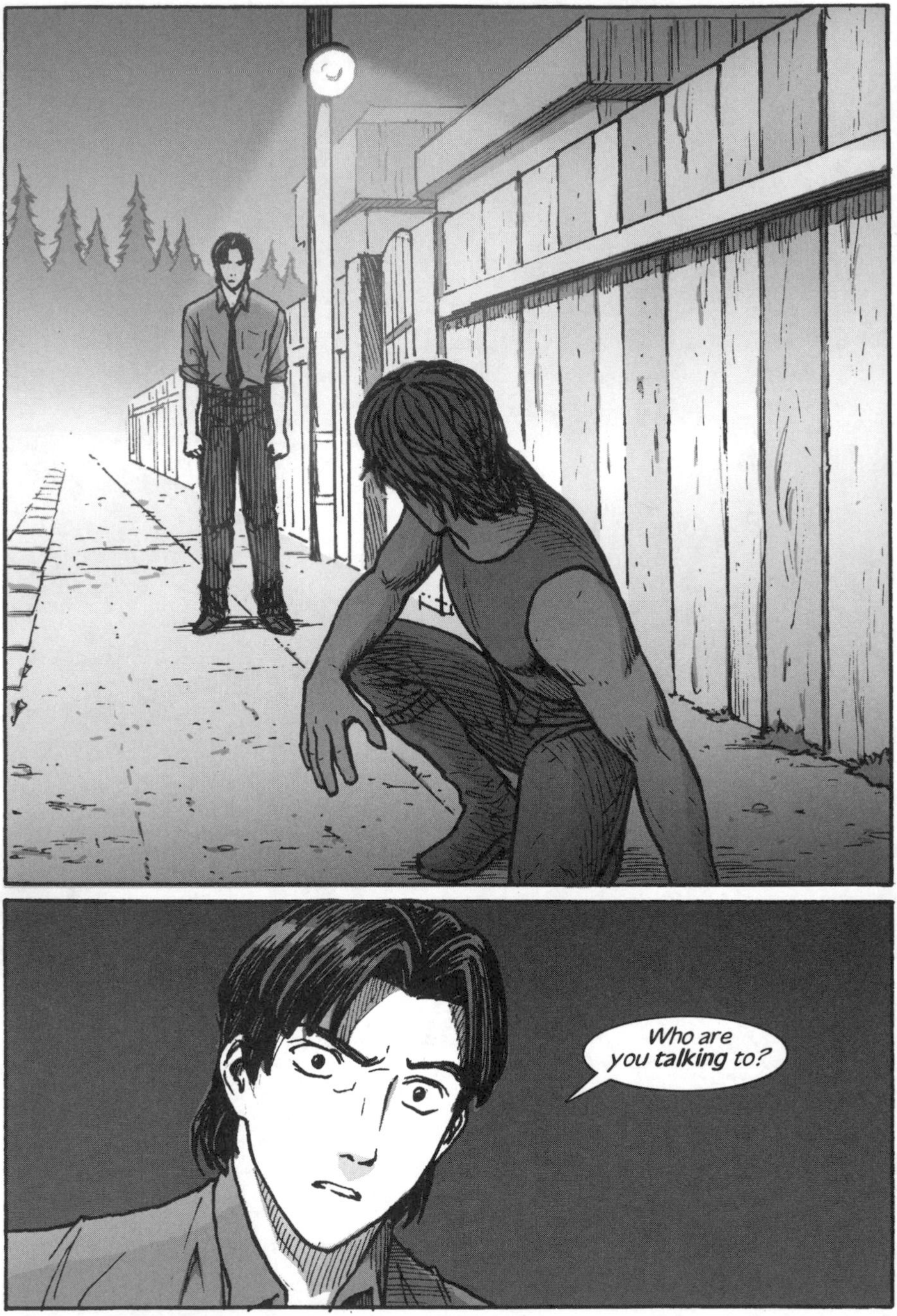
Who are
you talking to?

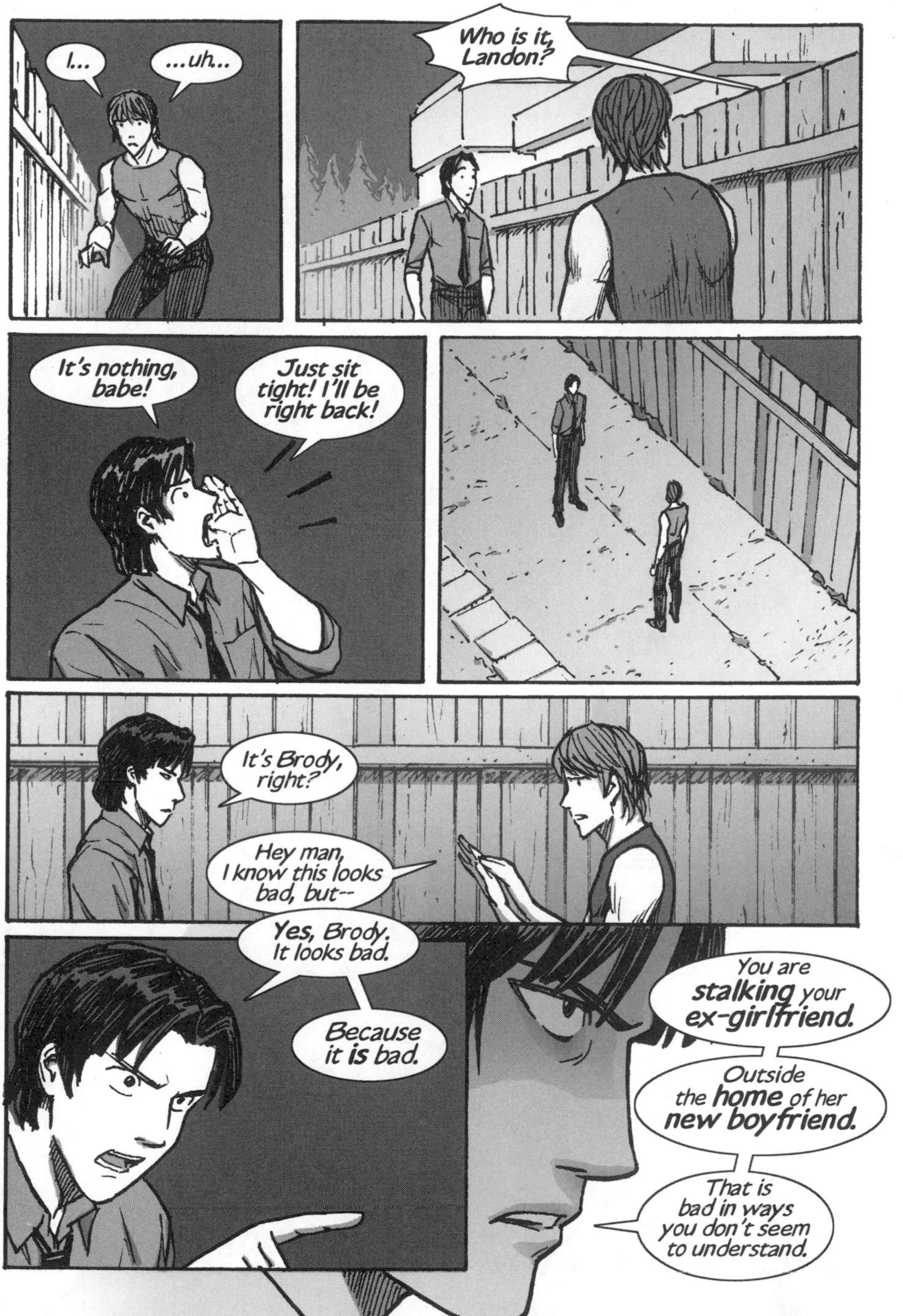
I...
...uh...
Who is it, Landon?
It's nothing, babe!
Just sit tight! I'll be right back!
It's Brody, right?
Hey man, I know this looks bad, but--
Yes, Brody. It looks bad.
Because it is bad.
You are stalking your ex-girlfriend.
Outside the home of her new boyfriend.
That is bad in ways you don't seem to understand.

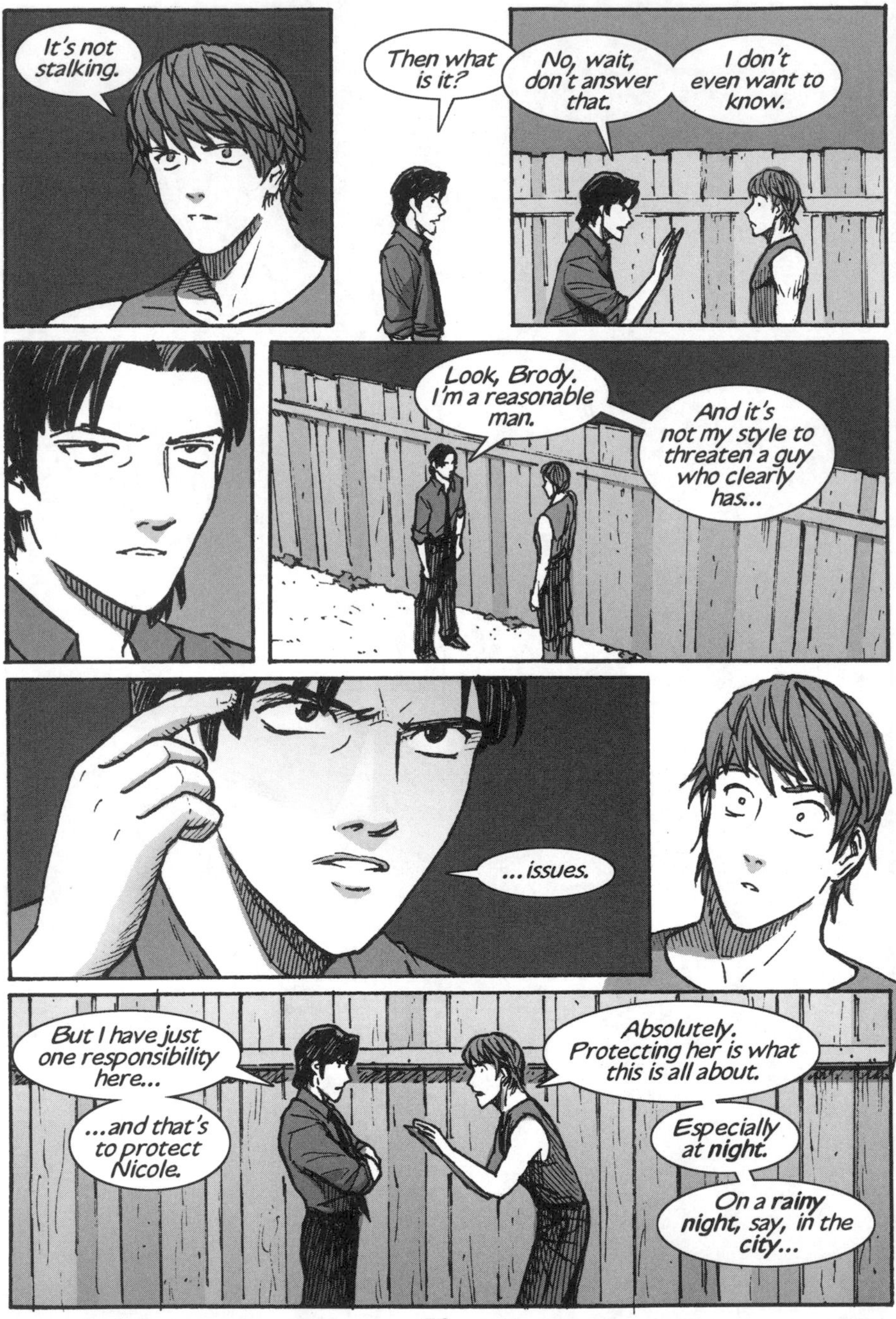
It's not stalking.
Then what is it?
No, wait, don't answer that.
I don't even want to know.
Look, Brody. I'm a reasonable man.
And it's not my style to threaten a guy who clearly has...
...issues.
But I have just one responsibility here...
...and that's to protect Nicole.
Absolutely. Protecting her is what this is all about.
Especially at **night**.
On a **rainy night**, say, in the **city**...

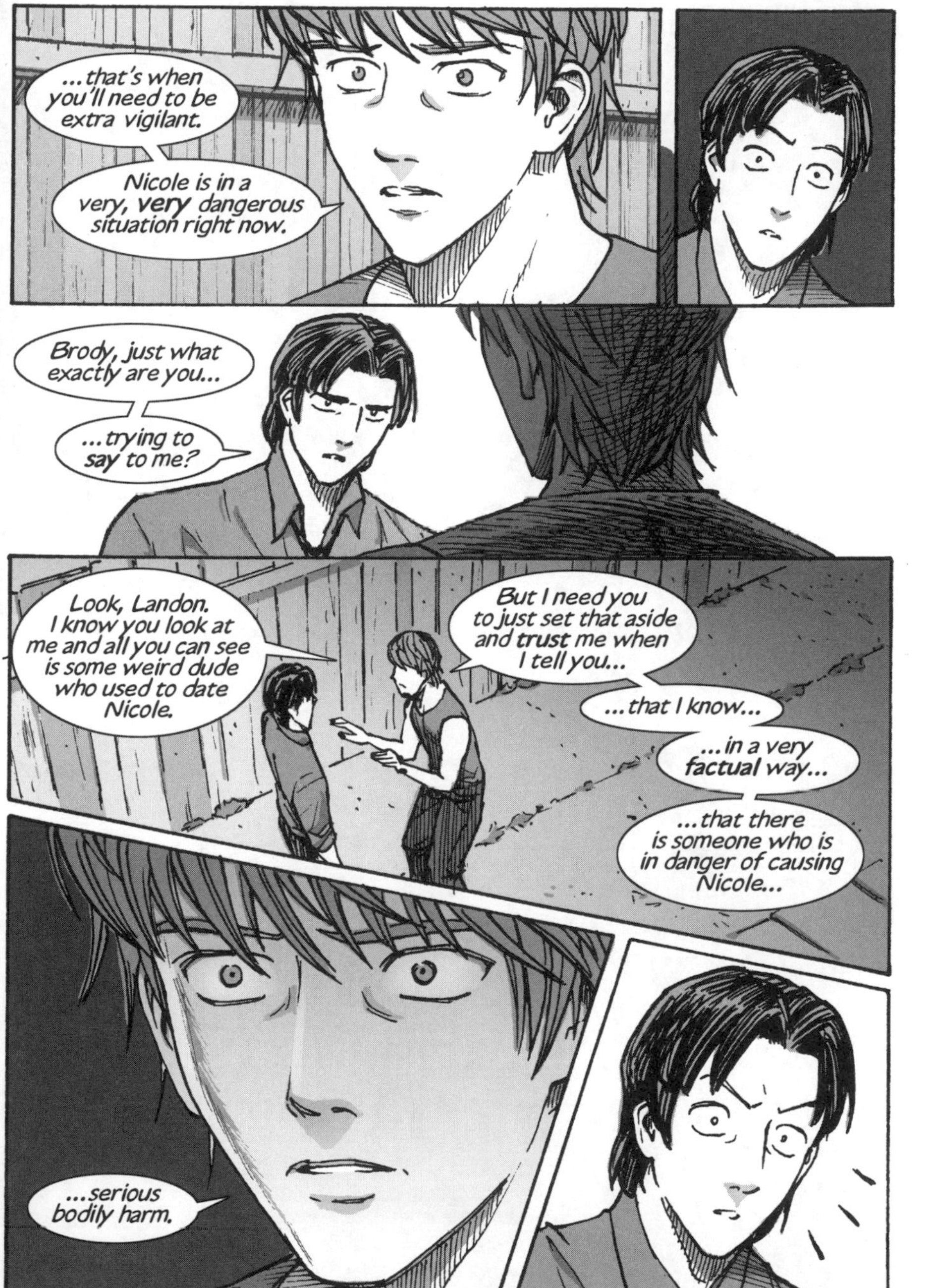
...that's when you'll need to be extra vigilant.
Nicole is in a very, very dangerous situation right now.
Brody, just what exactly are you...
...trying to say to me?
Look, Landon. I know you look at me and all you can see is some weird dude who used to date Nicole.
But I need you to just set that aside and trust me when I tell you...
...that I know...
...in a very factual way...
...that there is someone who is in danger of causing Nicole...
...serious bodily harm.

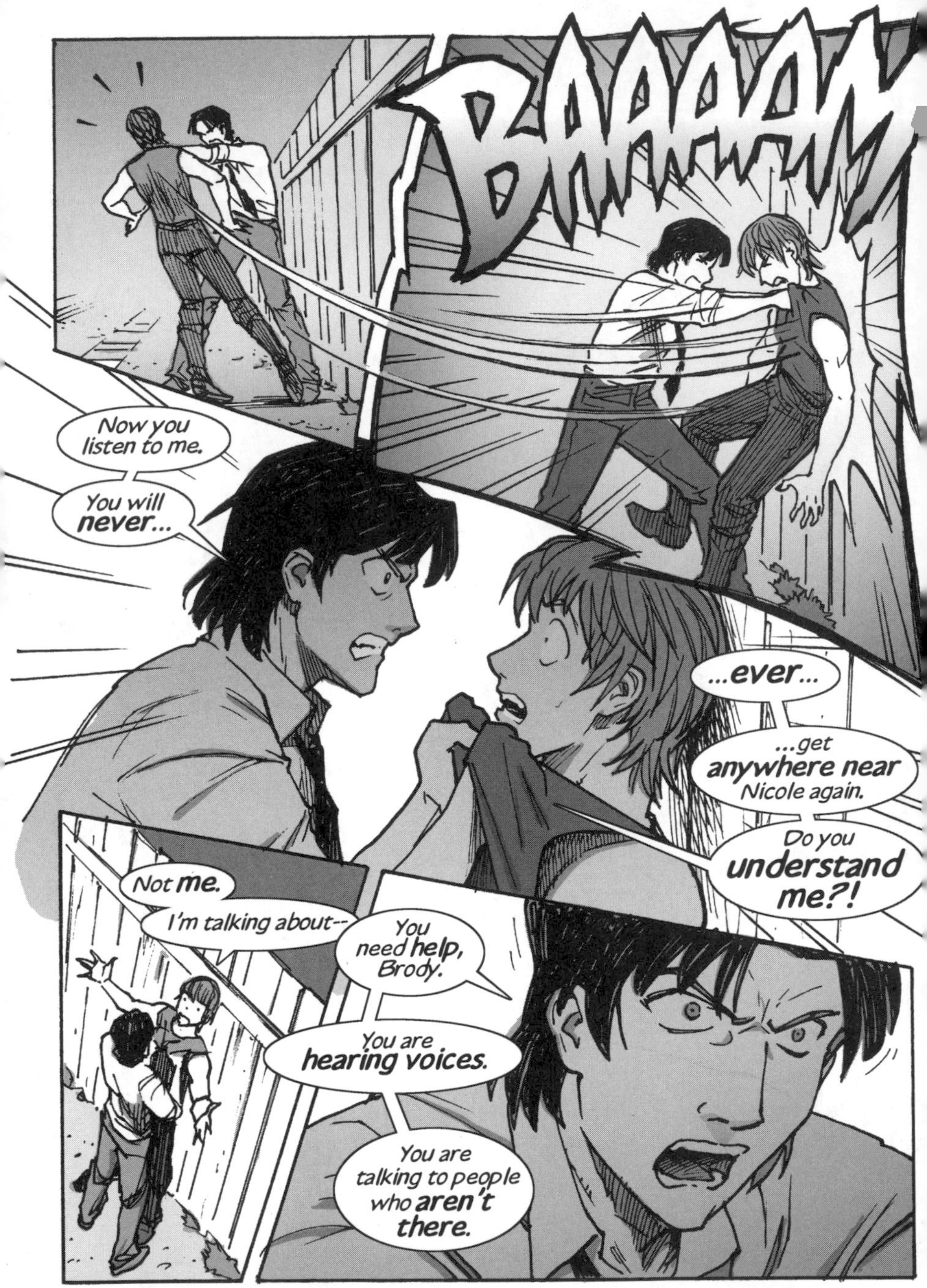
BAAAAM
Now you listen to me.
You will **never**...
...**ever**...
...get **anywhere near** Nicole again.
Do you **understand me?!**
Not **me.**
I'm talking about--
You need **help,** Brody.
You are **hearing voices.**
You are talking to people who **aren't there.**

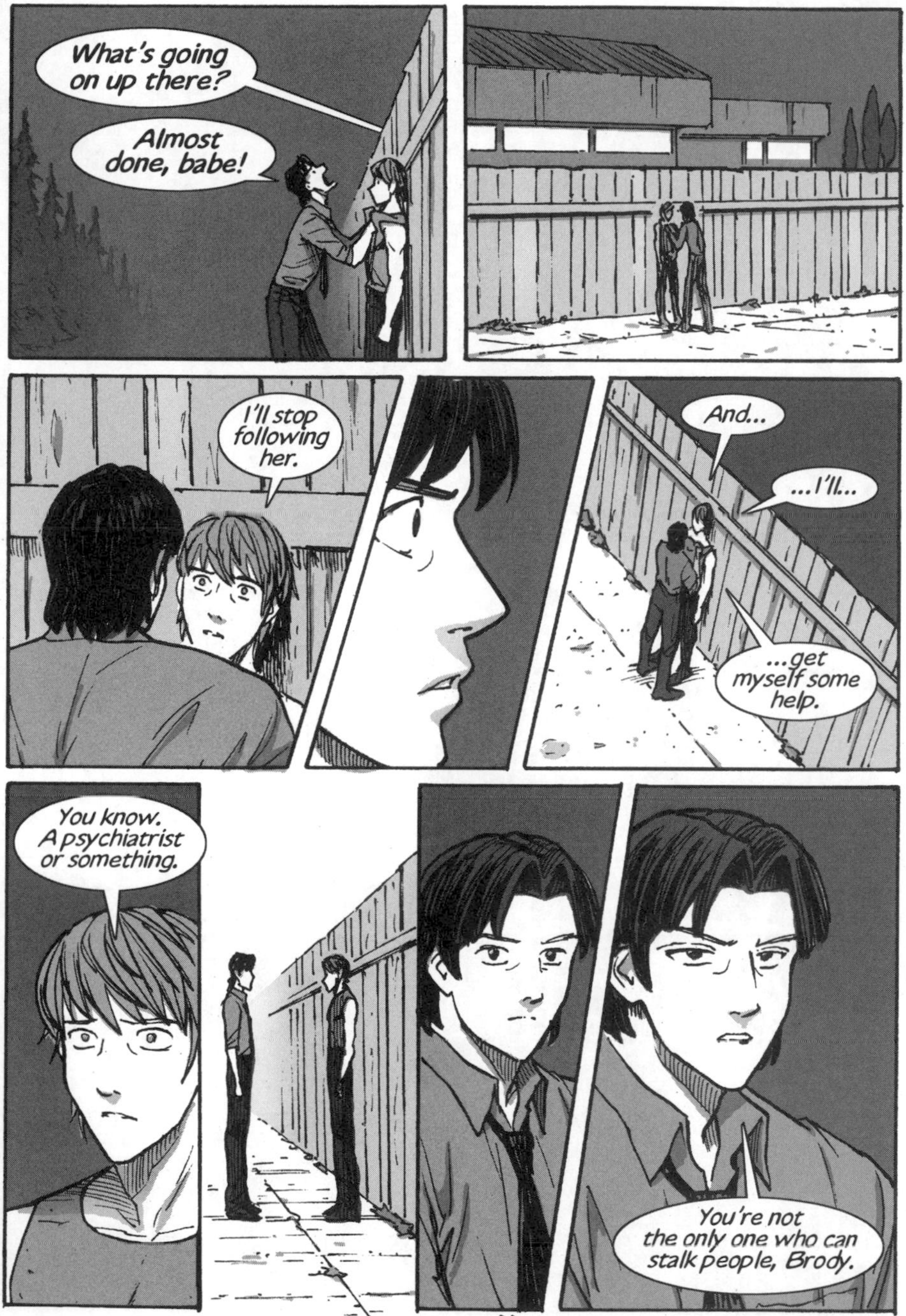
What's going on up there?
Almost done, babe!
I'll stop following her.
And...
...I'll...
...get myself some help.
You know. A psychiatrist or something.
You're not the only one who can stalk people, Brody.

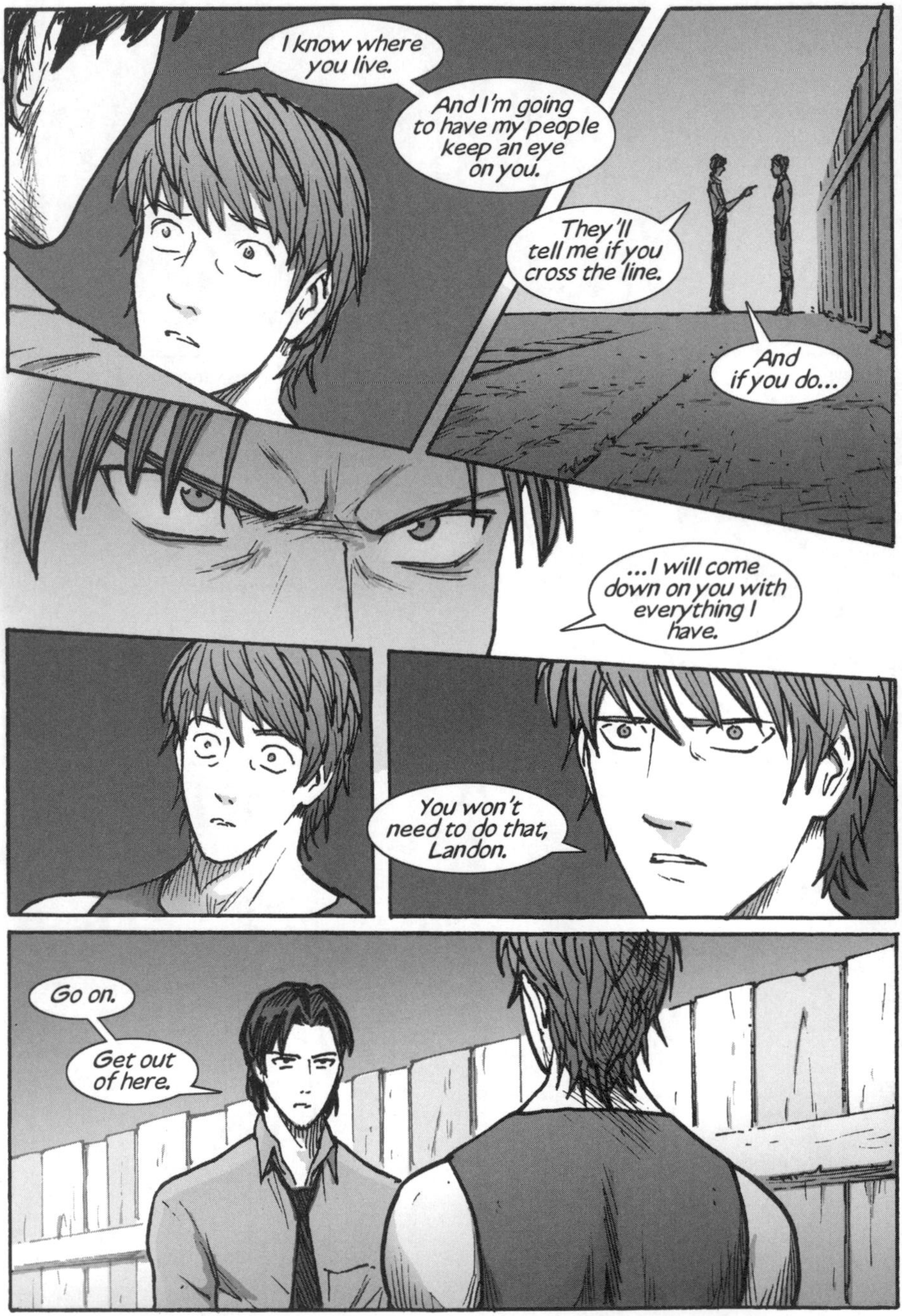
I know where you live.
And I'm going to have my people keep an eye on you.
They'll tell me if you cross the line.
And if you do...
...I will come down on you with everything I have.
You won't need to do that, Landon.
Go on.
Get out of here.

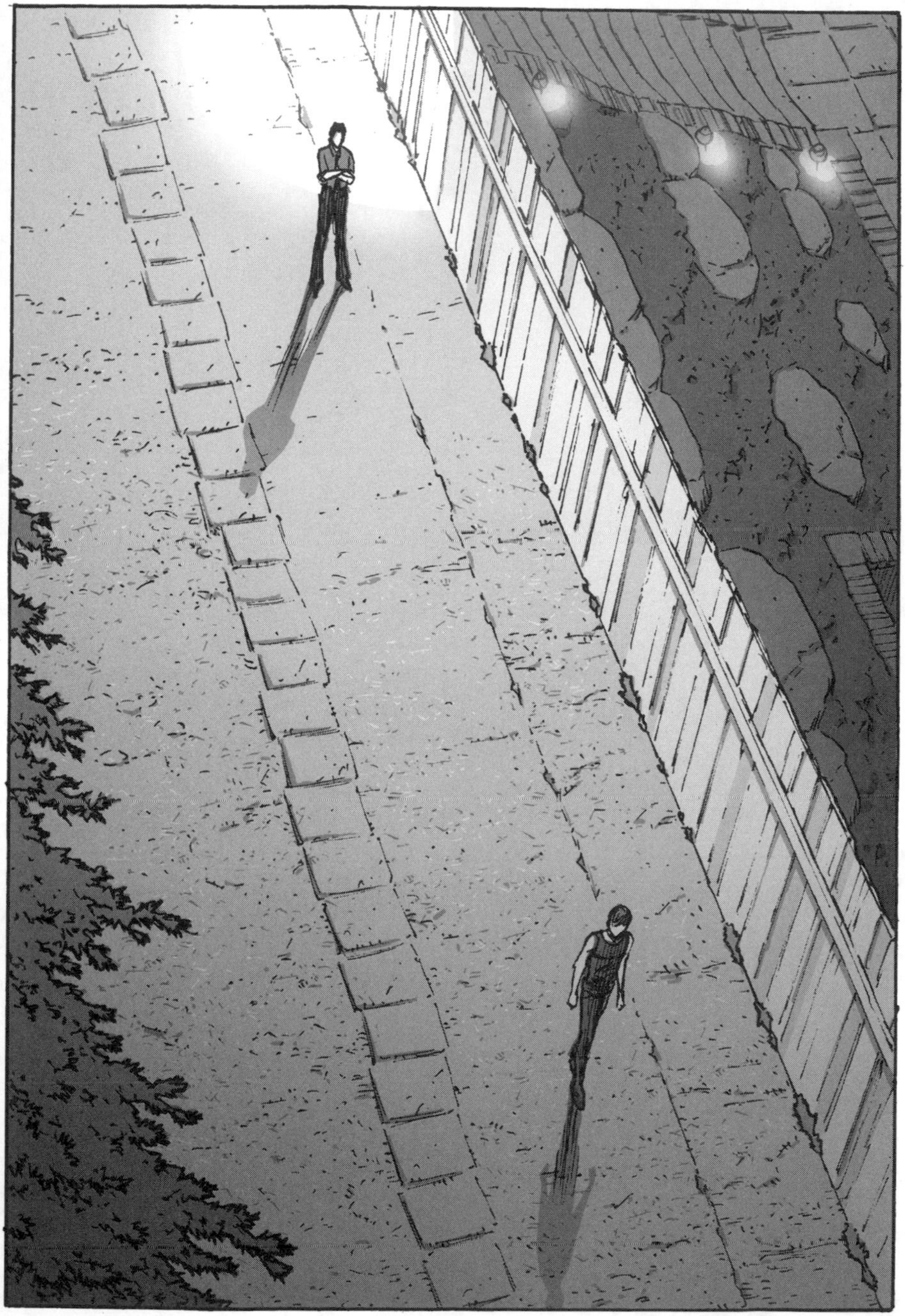

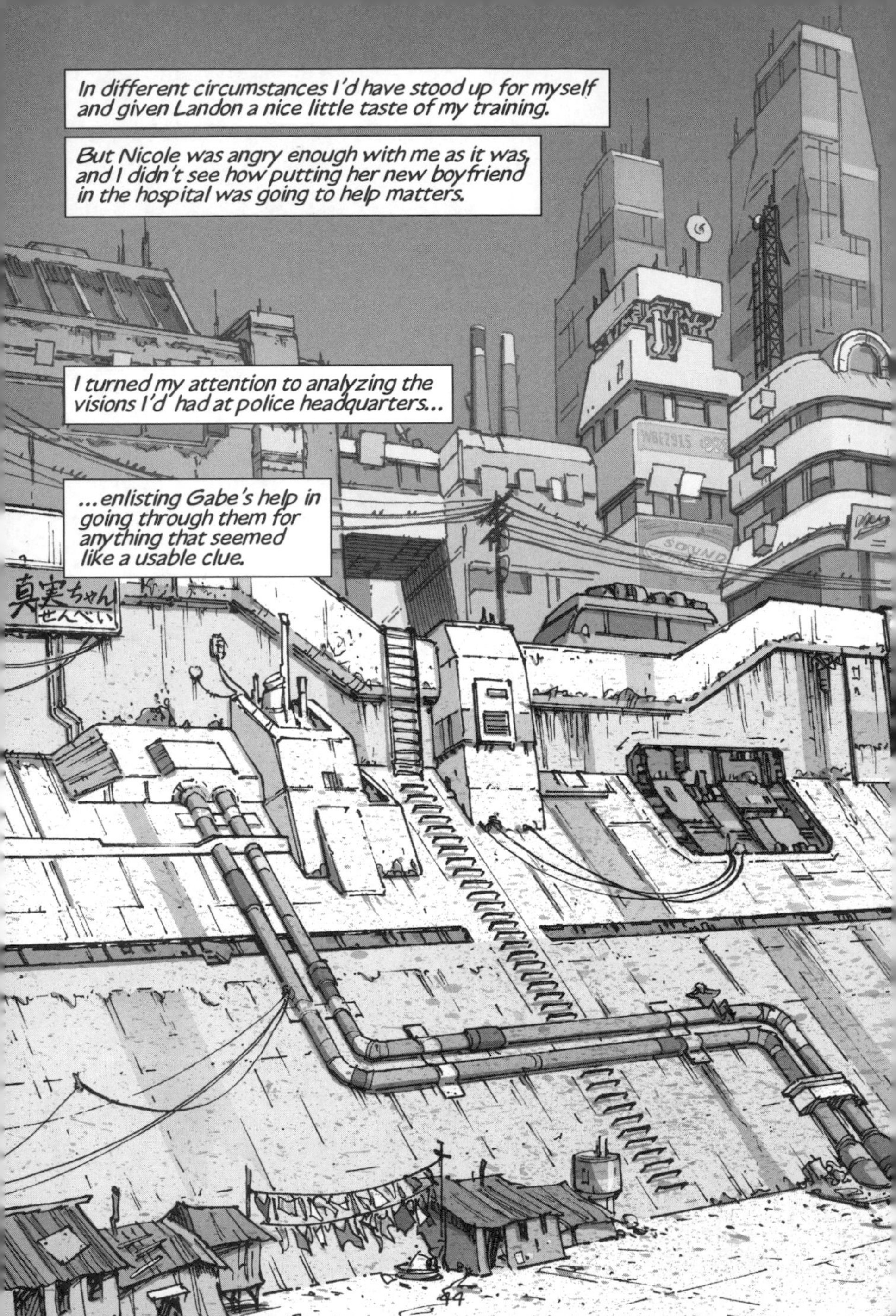
In different circumstances I'd have stood up for myself and given Landon a nice little taste of my training.
But Nicole was angry enough with me as it was, and I didn't see how putting her new boyfriend in the hospital was going to help matters.
I turned my attention to analyzing the visions I'd had at police headquarters...
...enlisting Gabe's help in going through them for anything that seemed like a usable clue.
真実ちゃん せんべい

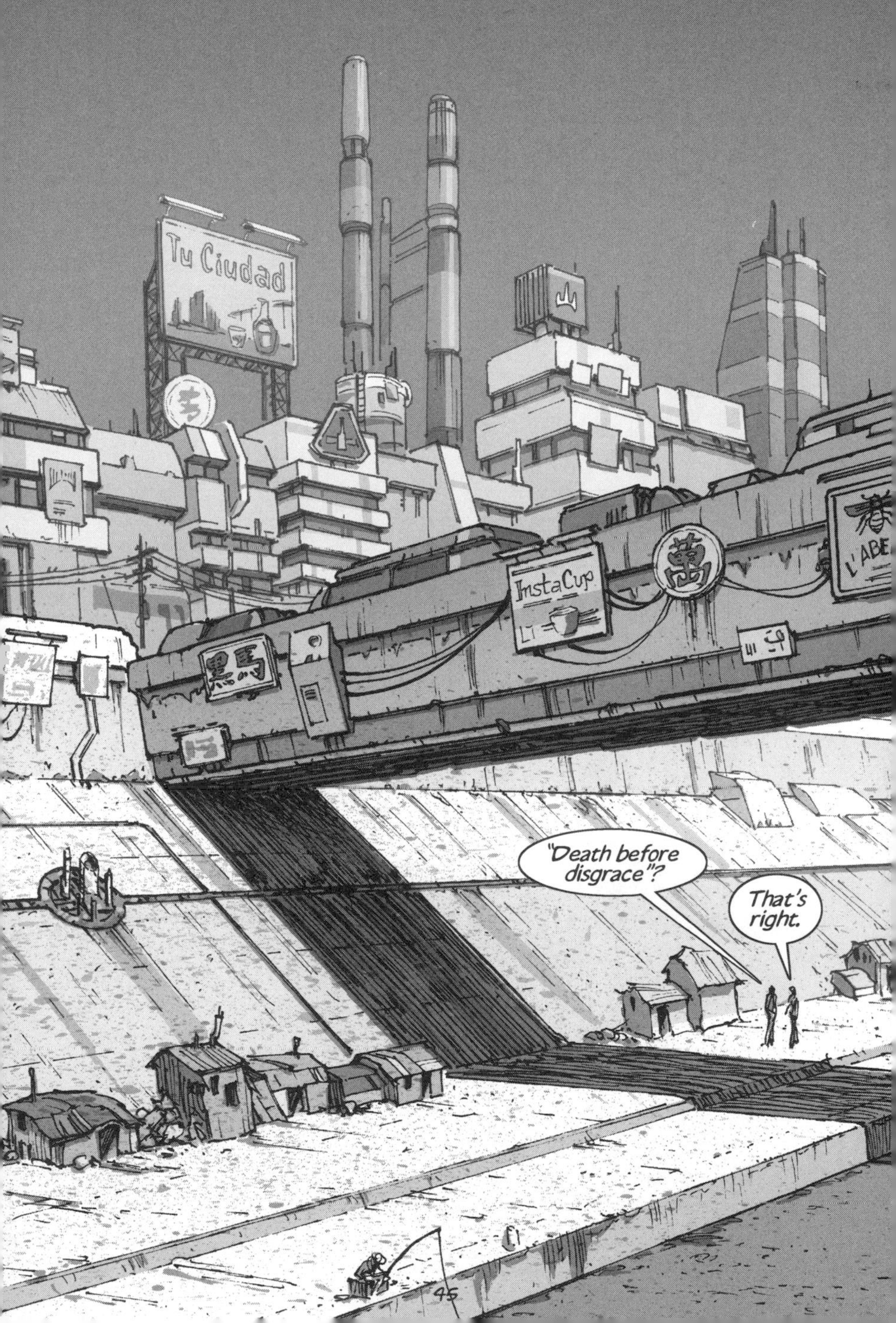
Tu Ciudad
InstaCup
"Death before disgrace"?
That's right.

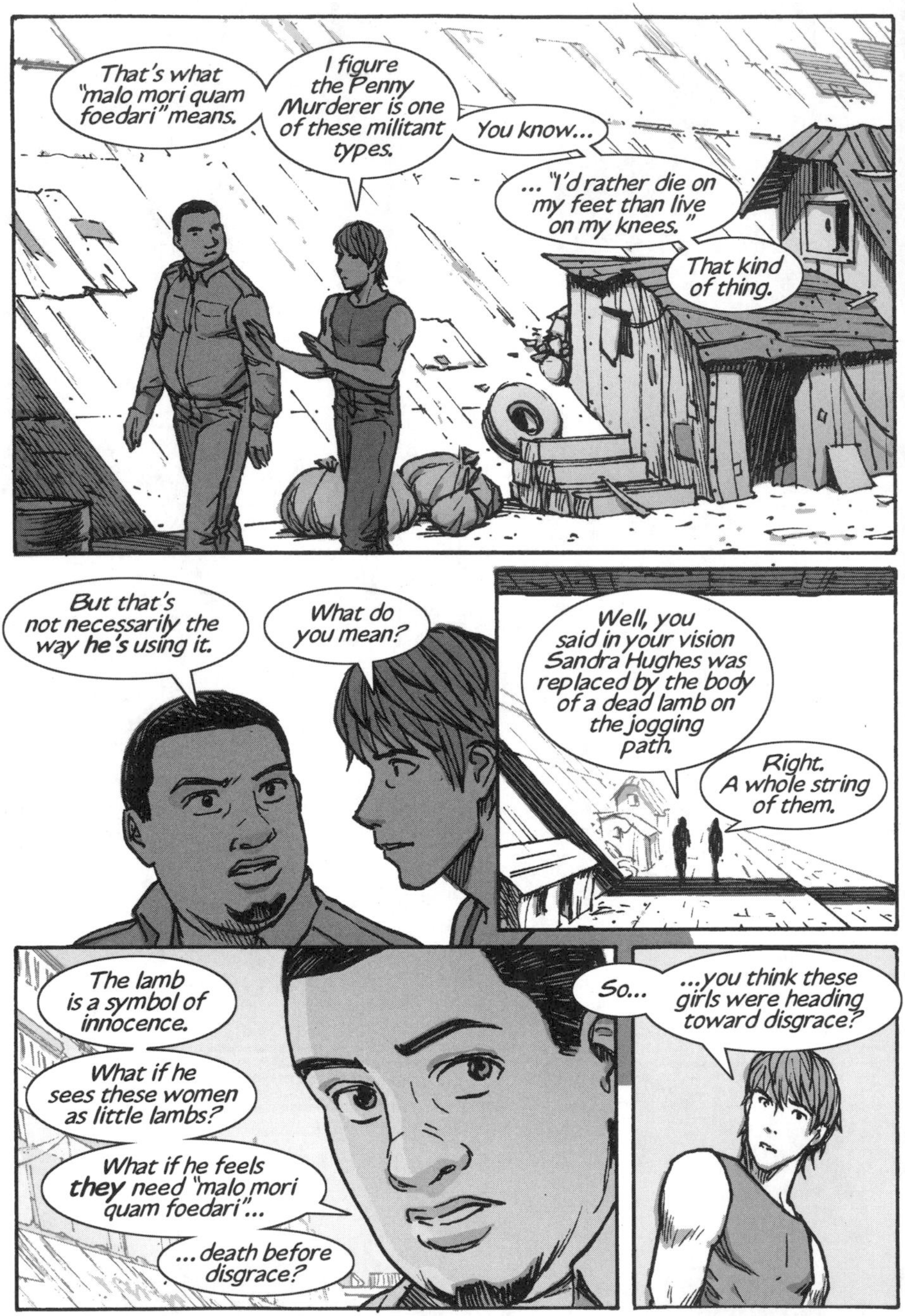
That's what "malo mori quam foedari" means.
I figure the Penny Murderer is one of these militant types.
You know...
... "I'd rather die on my feet than live on my knees."
That kind of thing.
But that's not necessarily the way he's using it.
What do you mean?
Well, you said in your vision Sandra Hughes was replaced by the body of a dead lamb on the jogging path.
Right. A whole string of them.
The lamb is a symbol of innocence.
What if he sees these women as little lambs?
What if he feels they need "malo mori quam foedari"...
... death before disgrace?
So...
...you think these girls were heading toward disgrace?

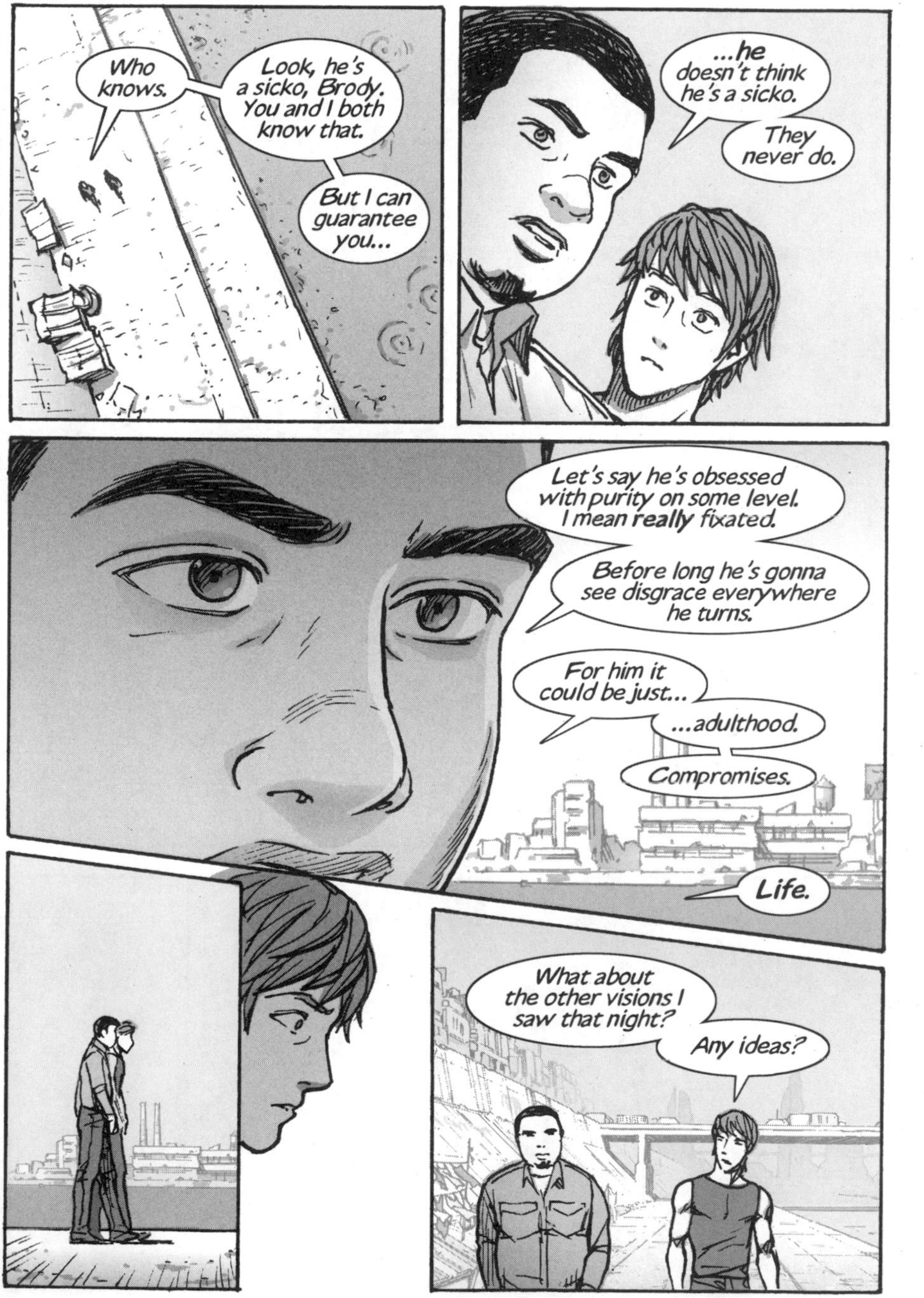
Who knows.
Look, he's a sicko, Brody. You and I both know that.
But I can guarantee you...
...he doesn't think he's a sicko.
They never do.
Let's say he's obsessed with purity on some level. I mean **really** fixated.
Before long he's gonna see disgrace everywhere he turns.
For him it could be just...
...adulthood.
Compromises.
Life.
What about the other visions I saw that night?
Any ideas?

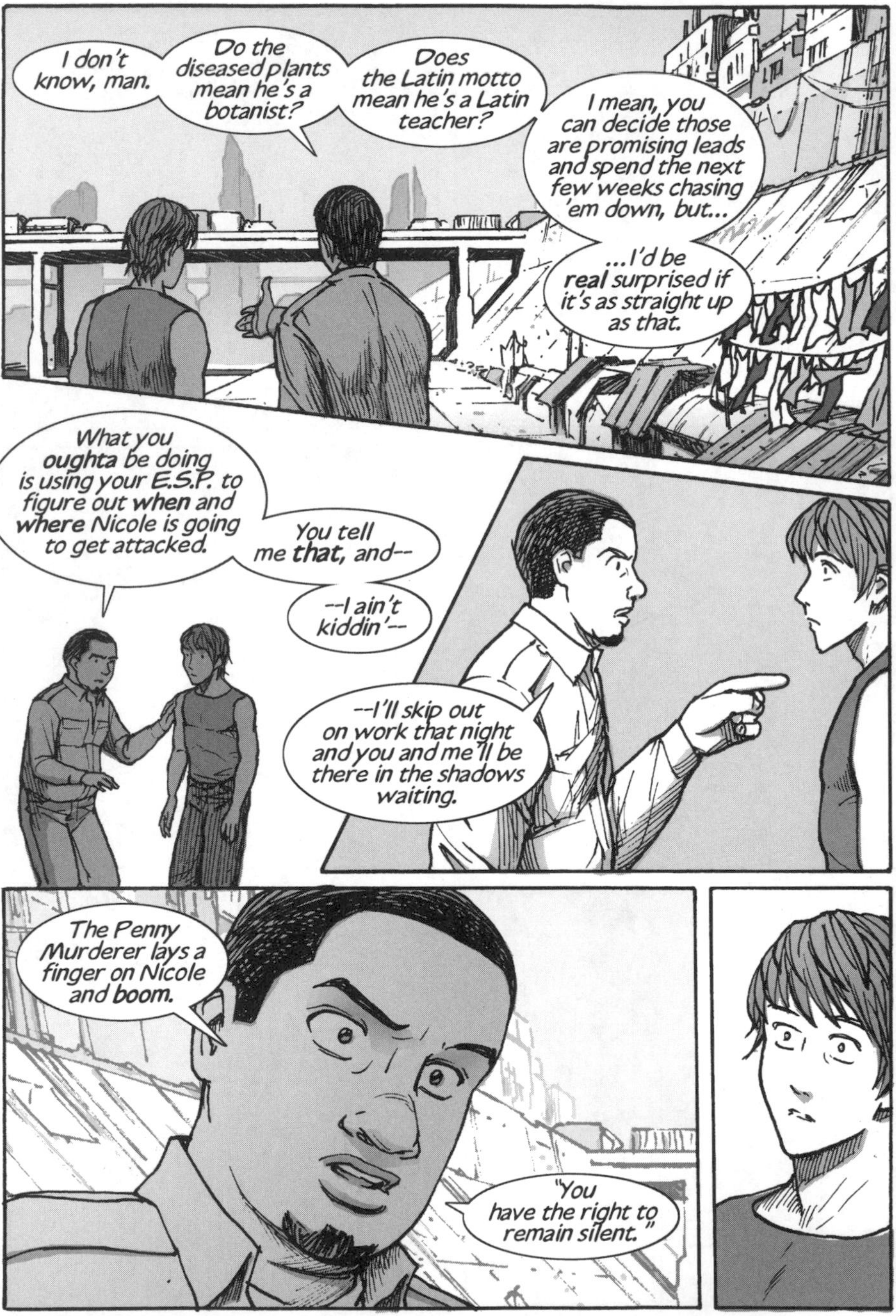
I don't know, man.
Do the diseased plants mean he's a botanist?
Does the Latin motto mean he's a Latin teacher?
I mean, you can decide those are promising leads and spend the next few weeks chasing 'em down, but...
...I'd be **real** surprised if it's as straight up as that.
What you **oughta** be doing is using your E.S.P. to figure out **when** and **where** Nicole is going to get attacked.
You tell me **that**, and--
--I ain't kiddin'--
--I'll skip out on work that night and you and me'll be there in the shadows waiting.
The Penny Murderer lays a finger on Nicole and **boom**.
"You have the right to remain silent."

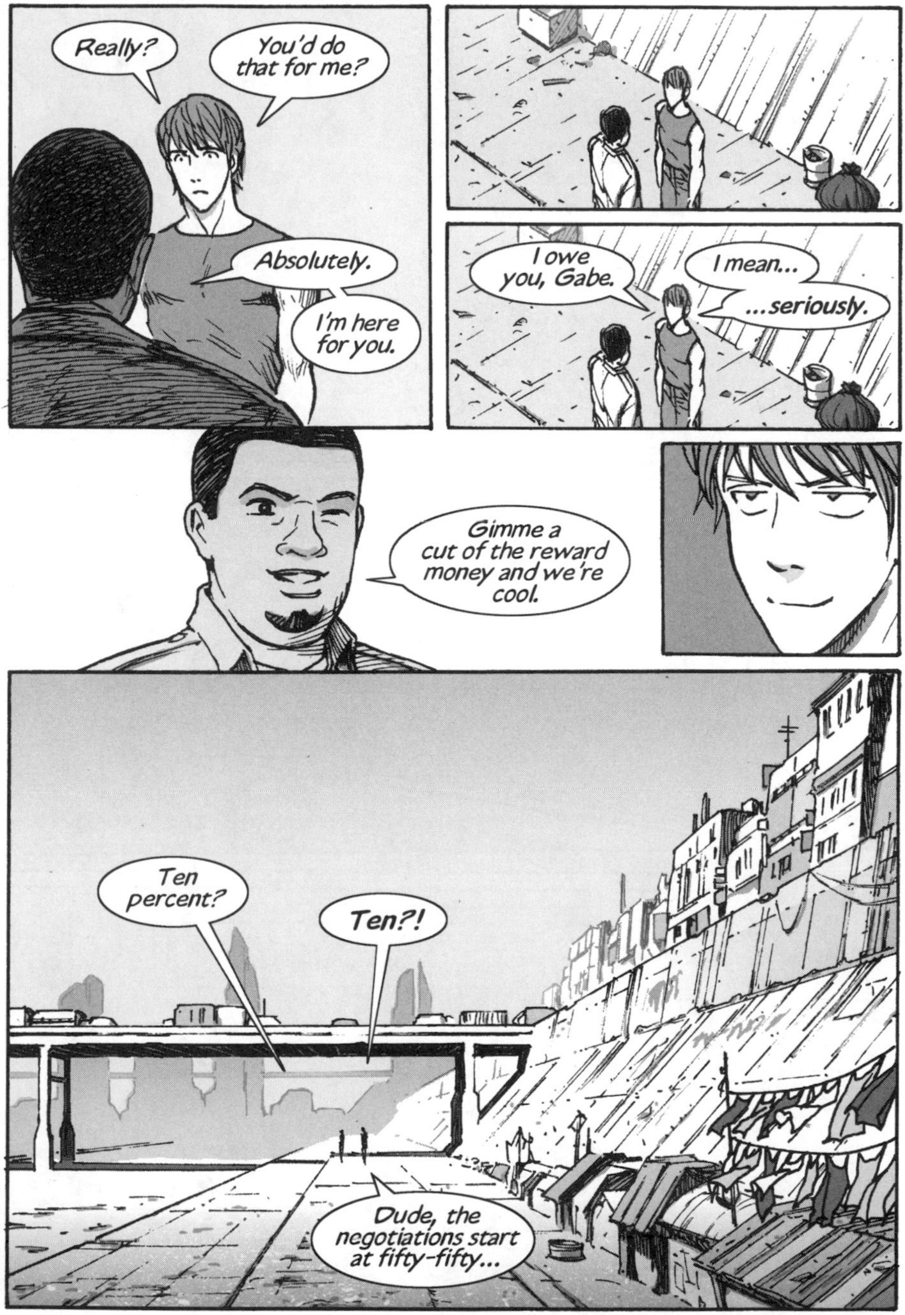
Really?
You'd do that for me?
Absolutely.
I'm here for you.
I owe you, Gabe.
I mean...
...seriously.
Gimme a cut of the reward money and we're cool.
Ten percent?
Ten?!
Dude, the negotiations start at fifty-fifty...

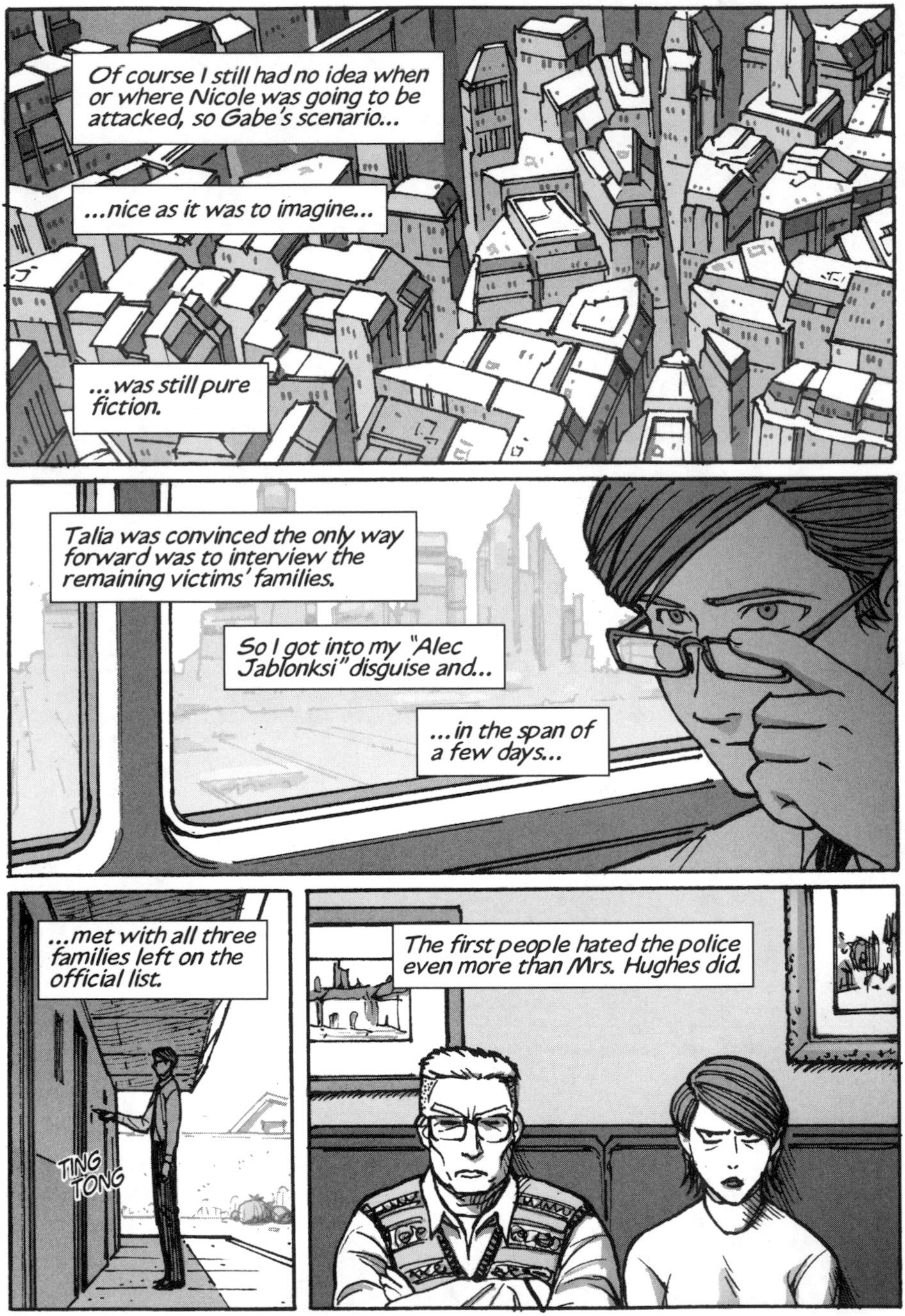
Of course I still had no idea when or where Nicole was going to be attacked, so Gabe's scenario...
...nice as it was to imagine...
...was still pure fiction.
Talia was convinced the only way forward was to interview the remaining victims' families.
So I got into my "Alec Jablonksi" disguise and...
...in the span of a few days...
...met with all three families left on the official list.
TING TONG
The first people hated the police even more than Mrs. Hughes did.

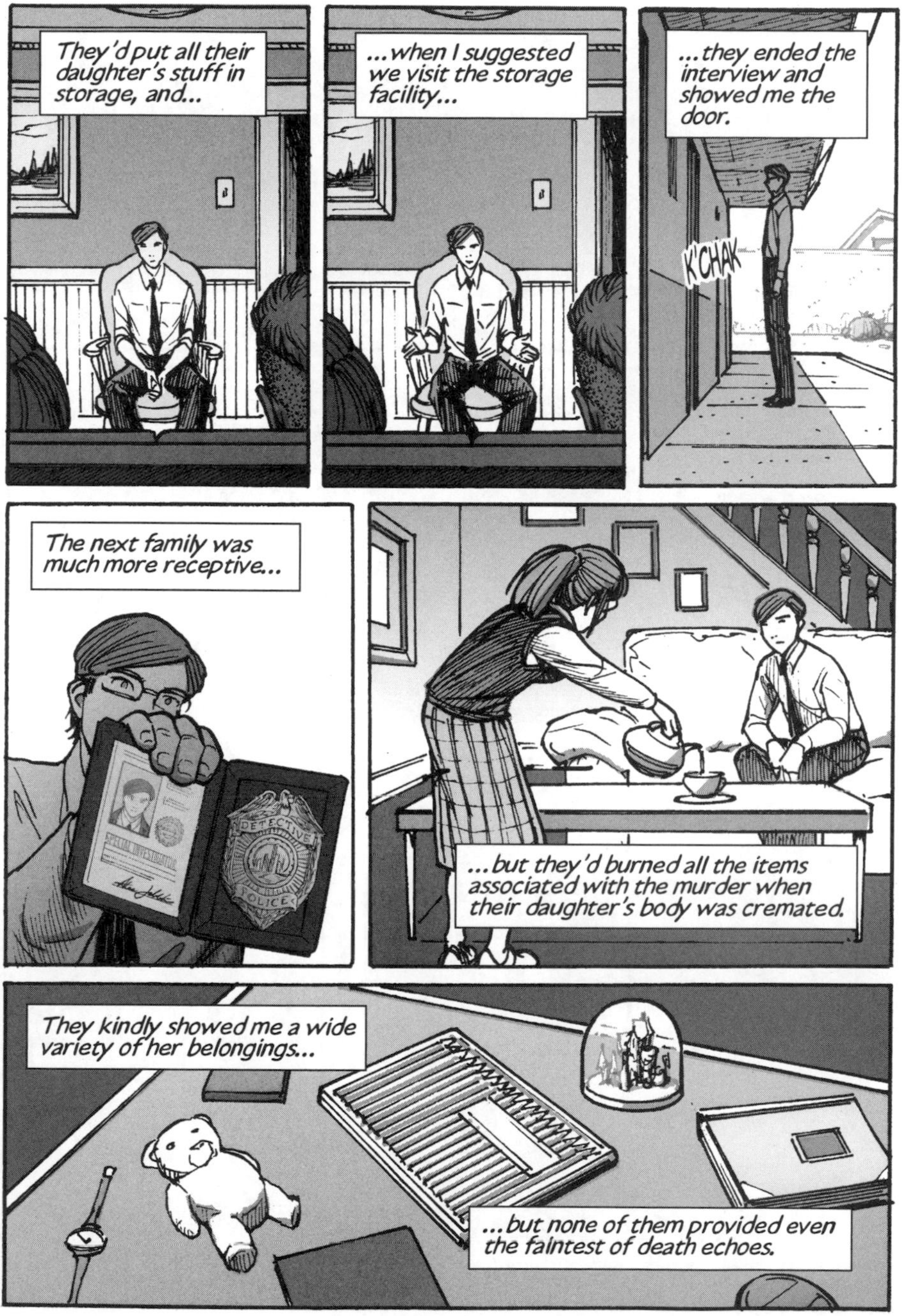
They'd put all their daughter's stuff in storage, and...
...when I suggested we visit the storage facility...
...they ended the interview and showed me the door.
K'CHAK
The next family was much more receptive...
DETECTIVE
POLICE
SPECIAL INVESTIGATION
...but they'd burned all the items associated with the murder when their daughter's body was cremated.
They kindly showed me a wide variety of her belongings...
...but none of them provided even the faintest of death echoes.

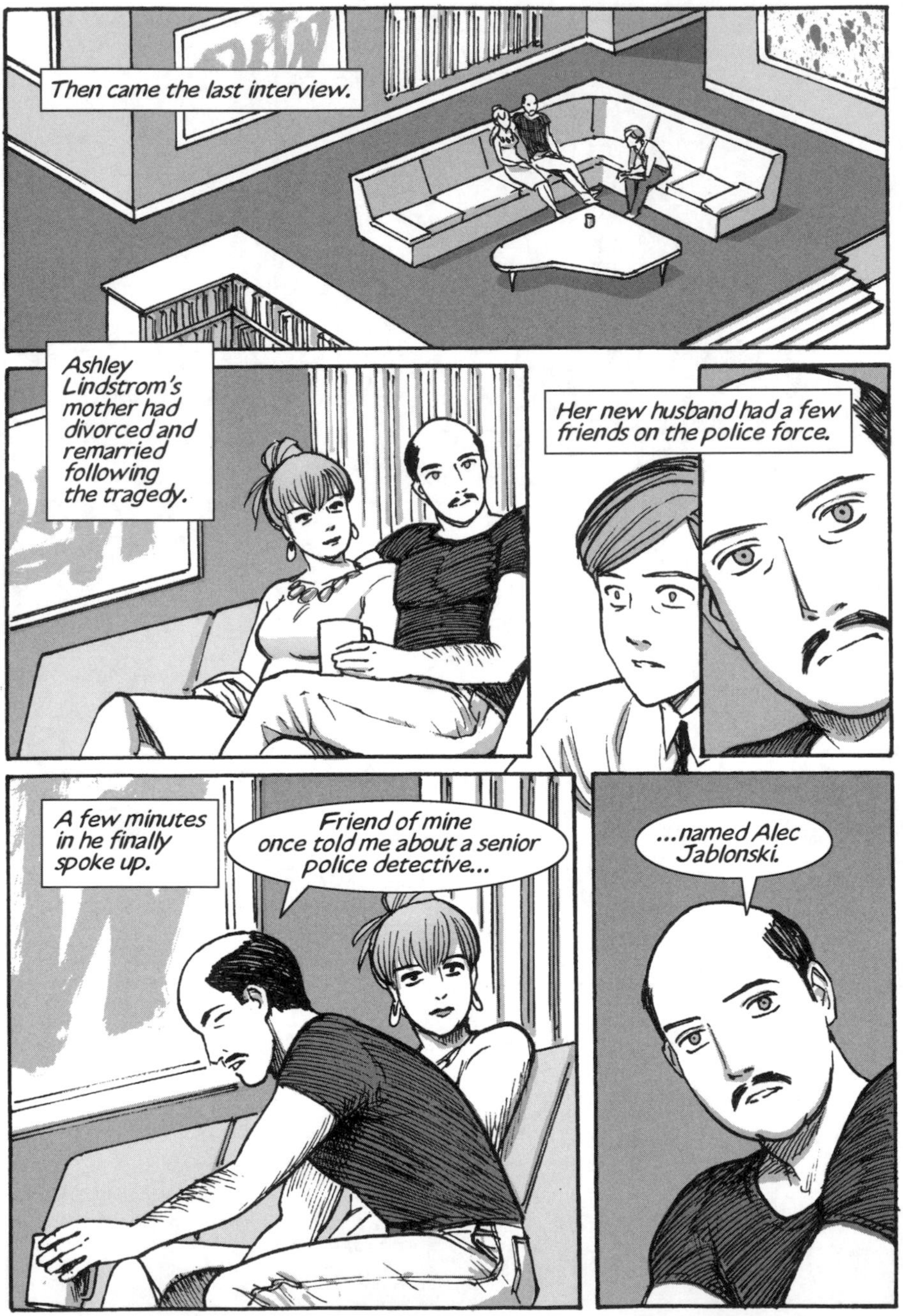

Then came the last interview.
Ashley Lindstrom's mother had divorced and remarried following the tragedy.
Her new husband had a few friends on the police force.
A few minutes in he finally spoke up.
Friend of mine once told me about a senior police detective...
...named Alec Jablonski.

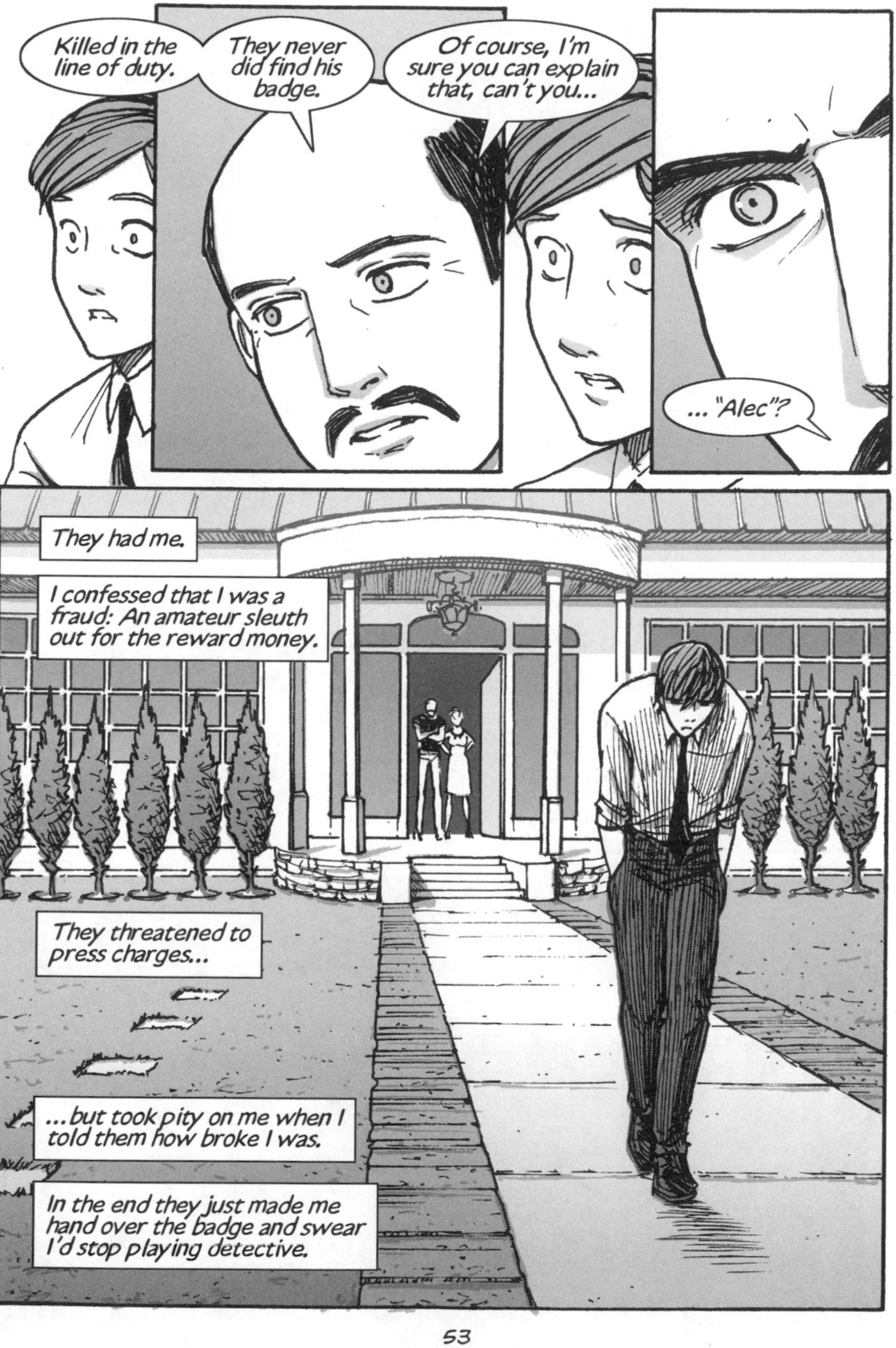
Killed in the line of duty.
They never did find his badge.
Of course, I'm sure you can explain that, can't you...
... "Alec"?
They had me.
I confessed that I was a fraud: An amateur sleuth out for the reward money.
They threatened to press charges...
...but took pity on me when I told them how broke I was.
In the end they just made me hand over the badge and swear I'd stop playing detective.

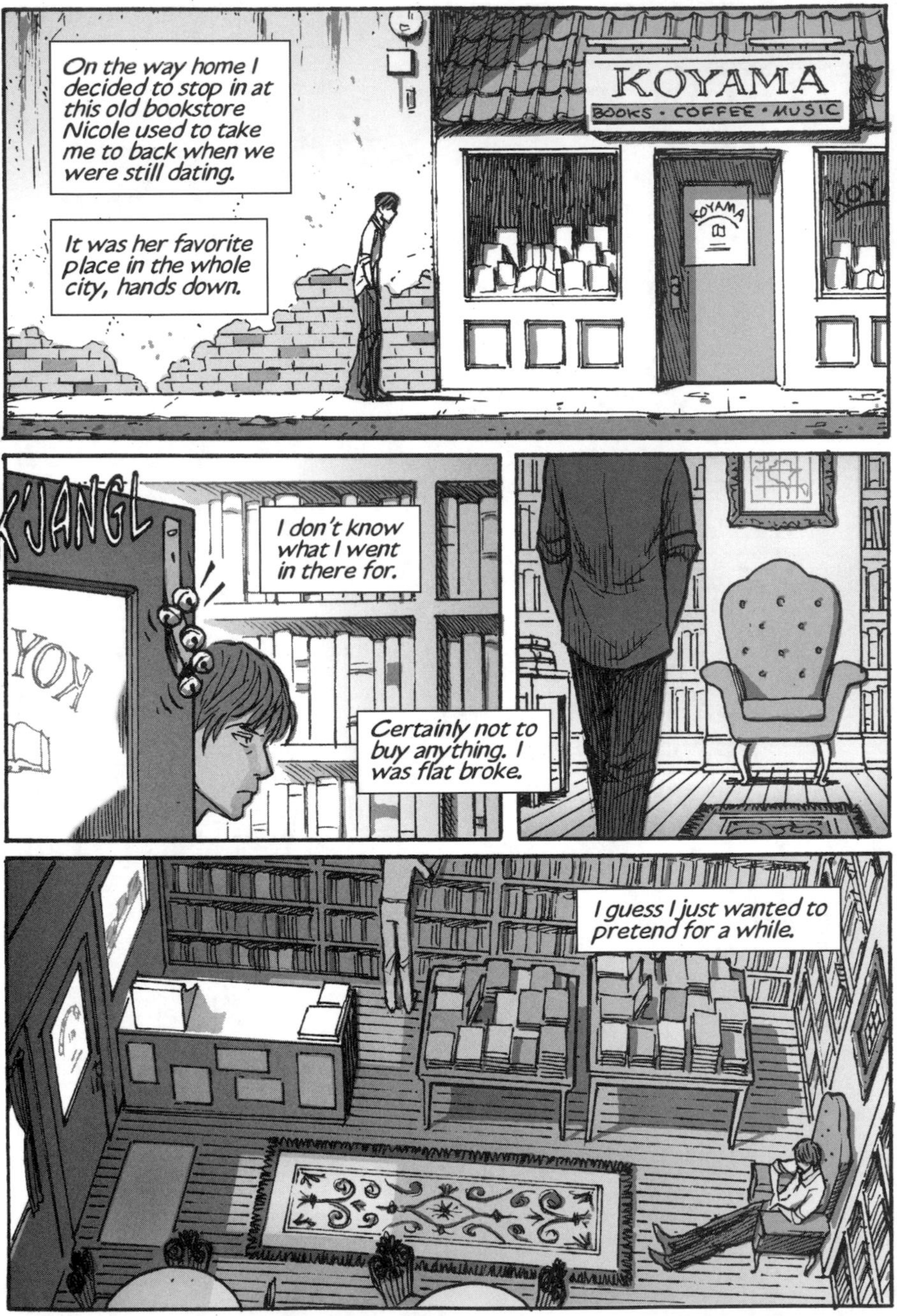
On the way home I decided to stop in at this old bookstore Nicole used to take me to back when we were still dating.
It was her favorite place in the whole city, hands down.
KOYAMA
BOOKS • COFFEE • MUSIC
KOYAMA
K'JANGL
I don't know what I went in there for.
Certainly not to buy anything. I was flat broke.
I guess I just wanted to pretend for a while.

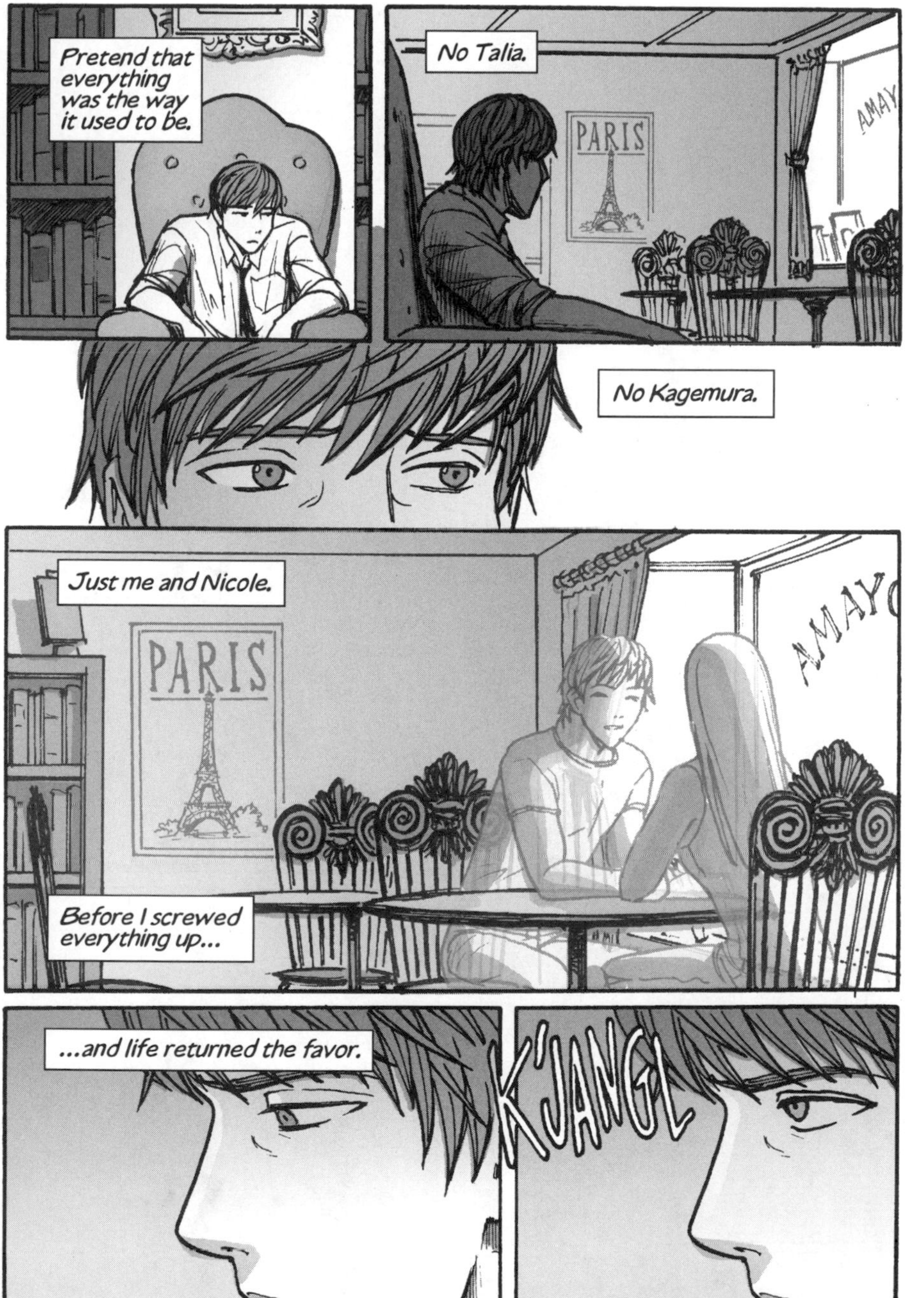

Pretend that everything was the way it used to be.
No Talia.
PARIS
AMAY
No Kagemura.
Just me and Nicole.
PARIS
AMAYO
Before I screwed everything up...
...and life returned the favor.
K'JANGL

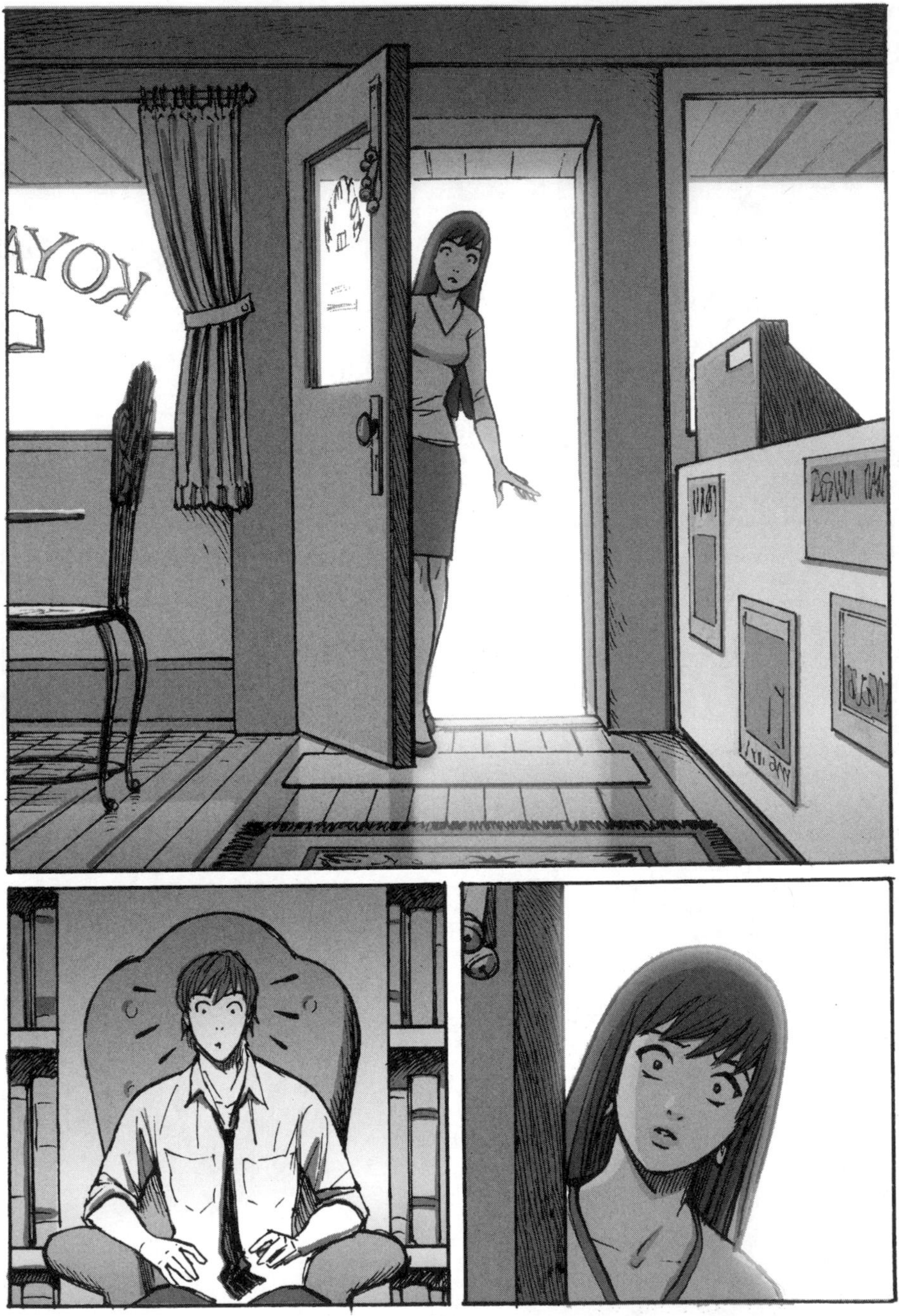

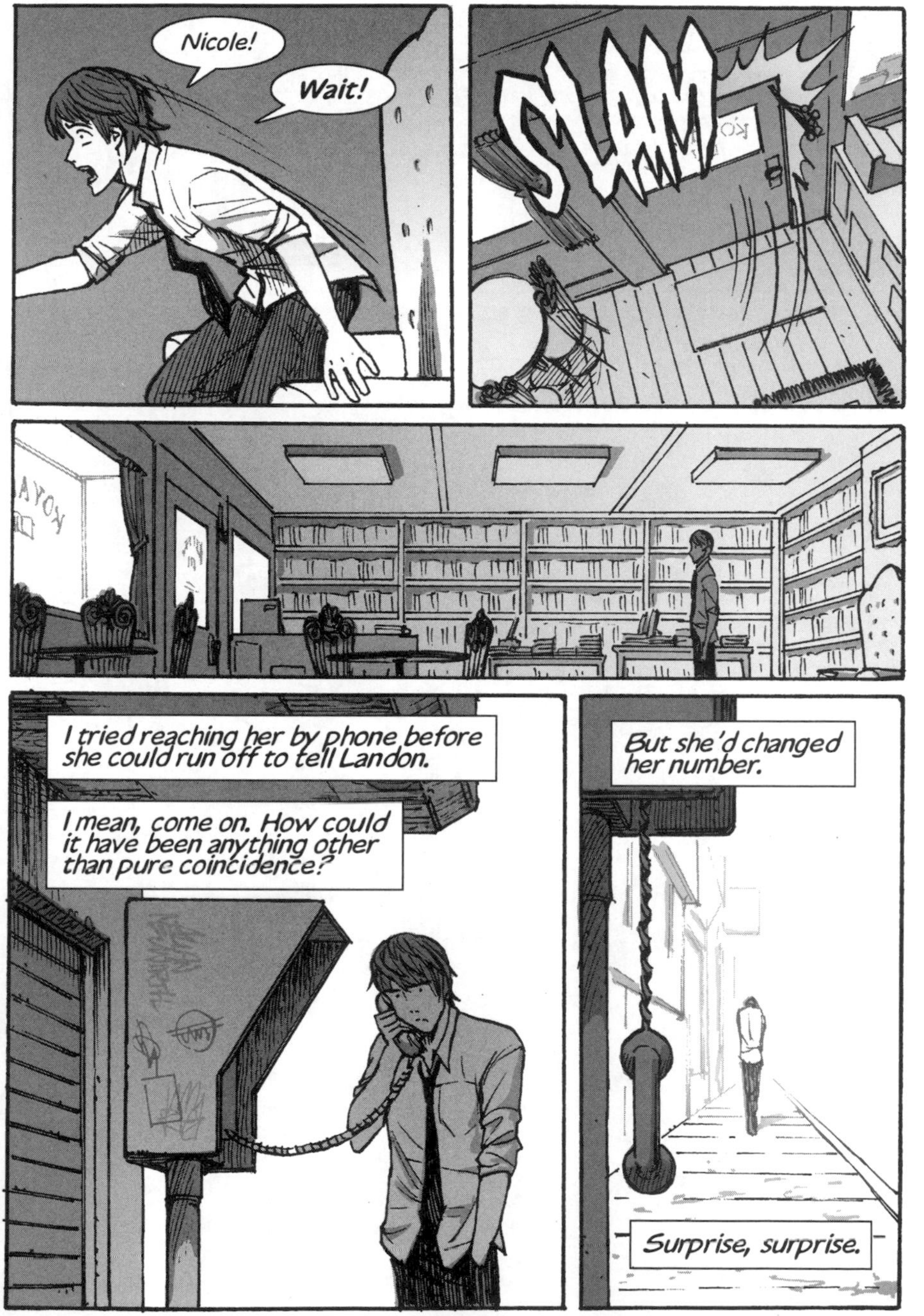
Nicole!
Wait!
SLAM
I tried reaching her by phone before she could run off to tell Landon.
I mean, come on. How could it have been anything other than pure coincidence?
But she'd changed her number.
Surprise, surprise.

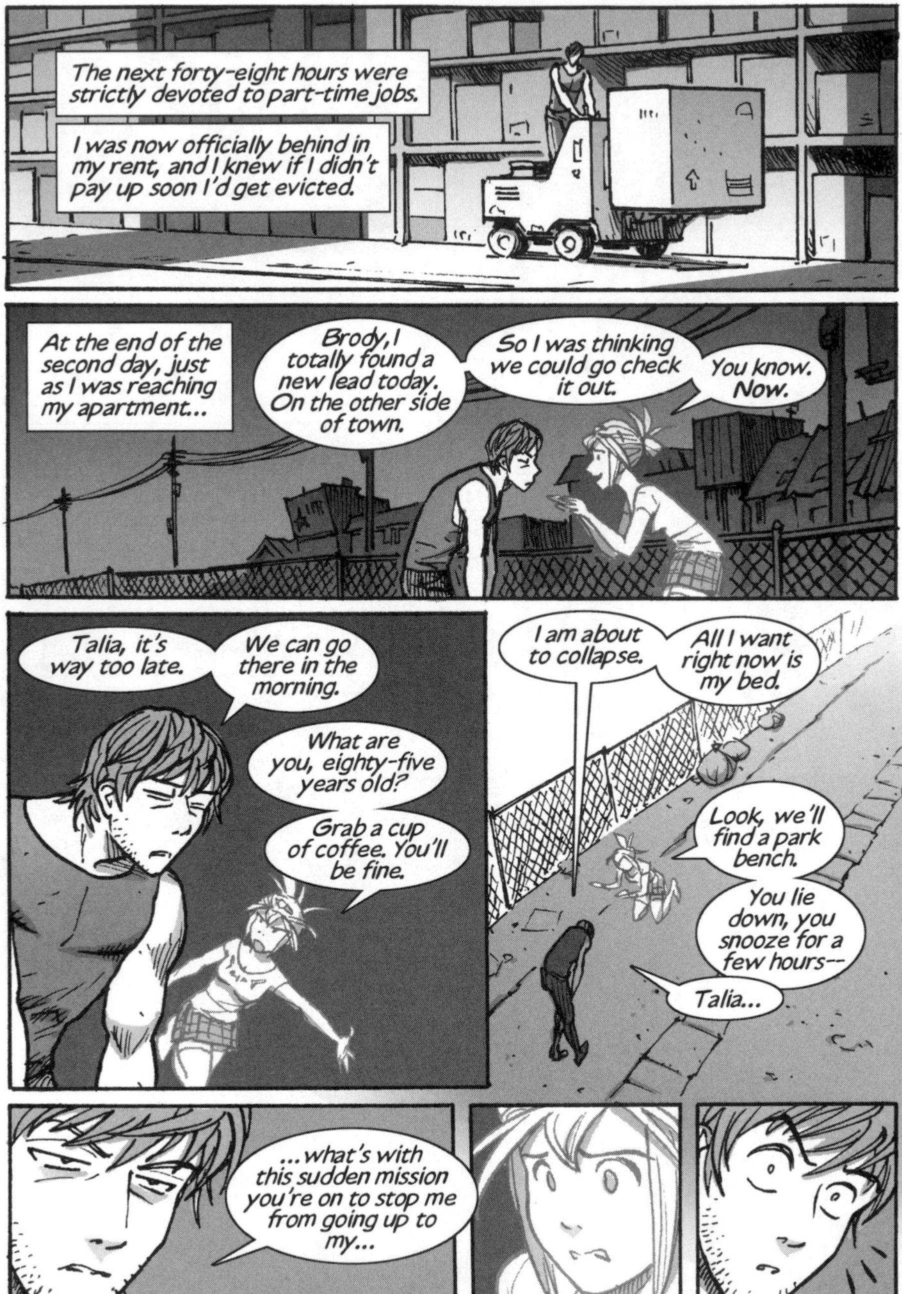
The next forty-eight hours were strictly devoted to part-time jobs.
I was now officially behind in my rent, and I knew if I didn't pay up soon I'd get evicted.
At the end of the second day, just as I was reaching my apartment...
Brody, I totally found a new lead today. On the other side of town.
So I was thinking we could go check it out.
You know. Now.
Talia, it's way too late.
We can go there in the morning.
What are you, eighty-five years old?
Grab a cup of coffee. You'll be fine.
I am about to collapse.
All I want right now is my bed.
Look, we'll find a park bench.
You lie down, you snooze for a few hours--
Talia...
...what's with this sudden mission you're on to stop me from going up to my...

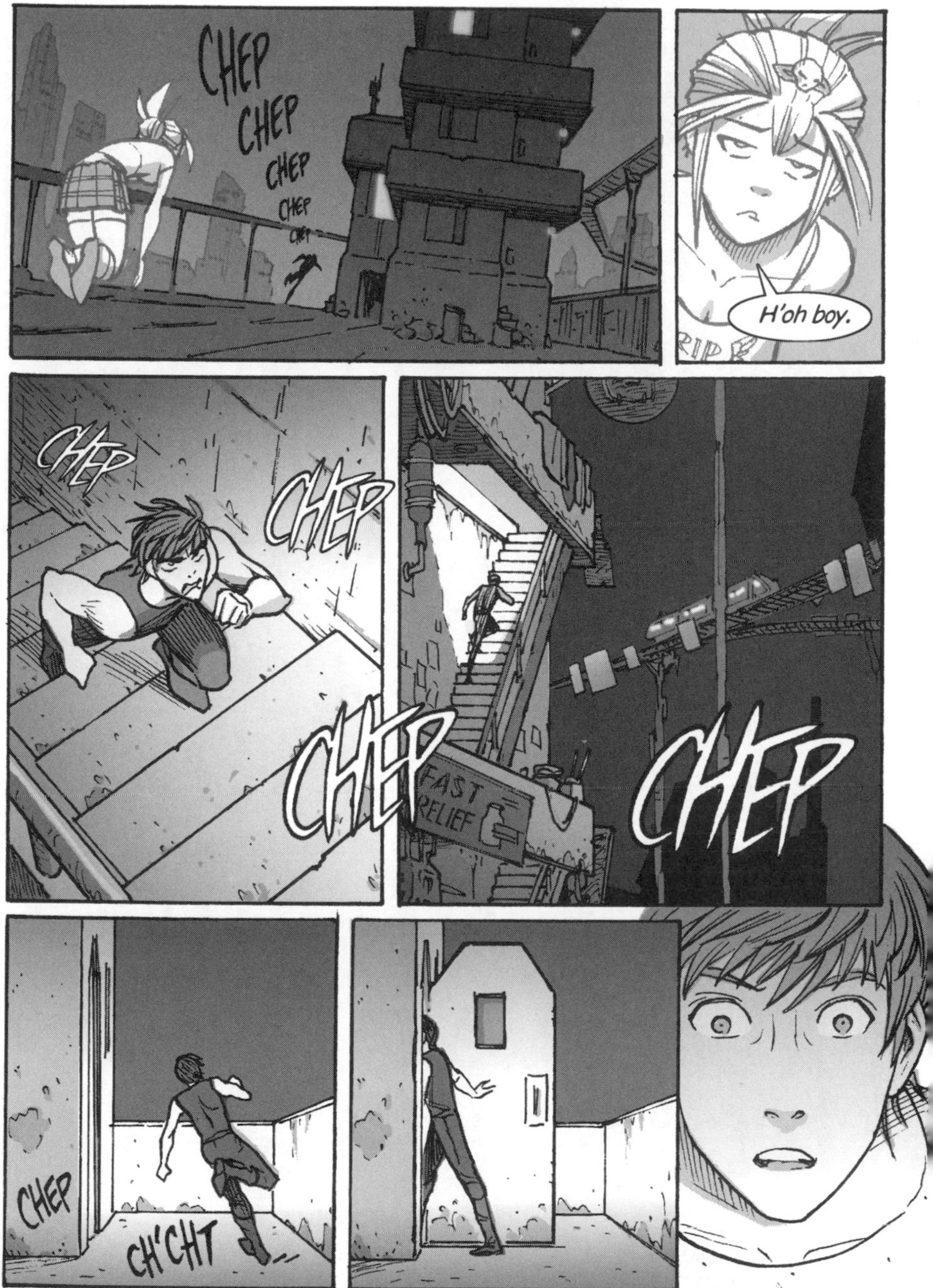
CHEP
CHEP
CHEP
CHEP
CHEP
H'oh boy.
CHEP
CHEP
CHEP
CHEP
FAST RELIEF
CHEP
CH'CHT

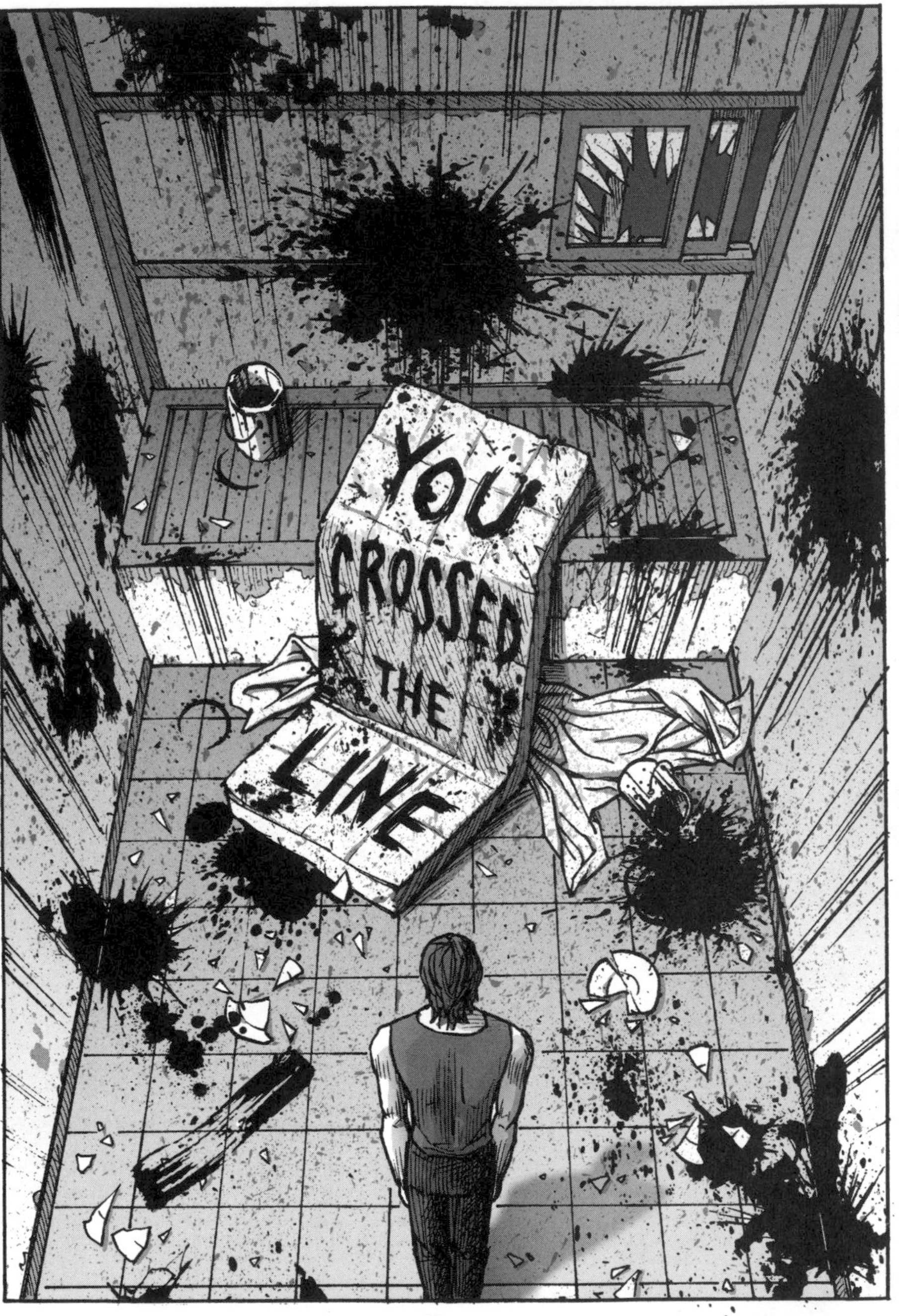
YOU CROSSED THE LINE

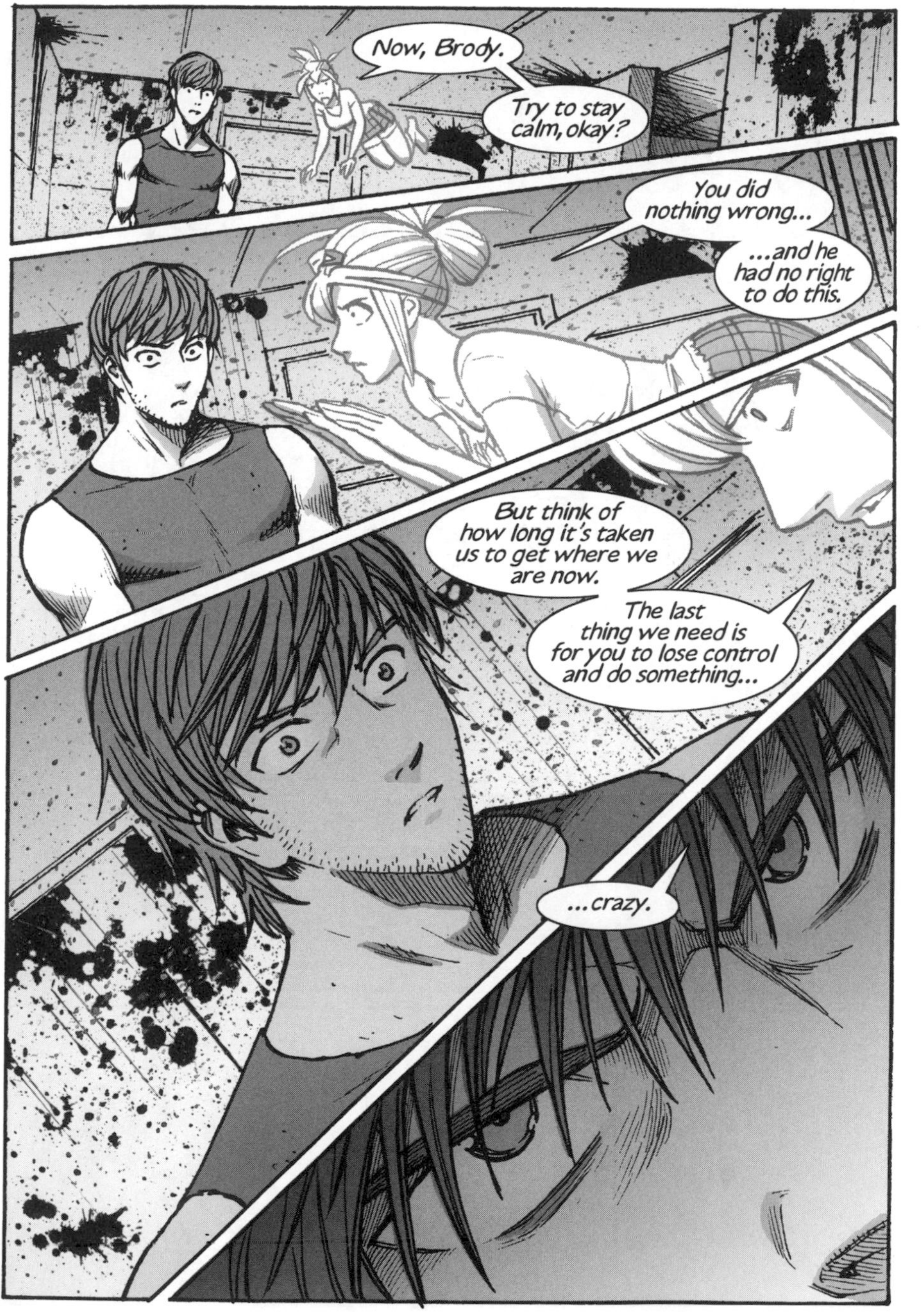
Now, Brody.
Try to stay calm, okay?
You did nothing wrong...
...and he had no right to do this.
But think of how long it's taken us to get where we are now.
The last thing we need is for you to lose control and do something...
...crazy.

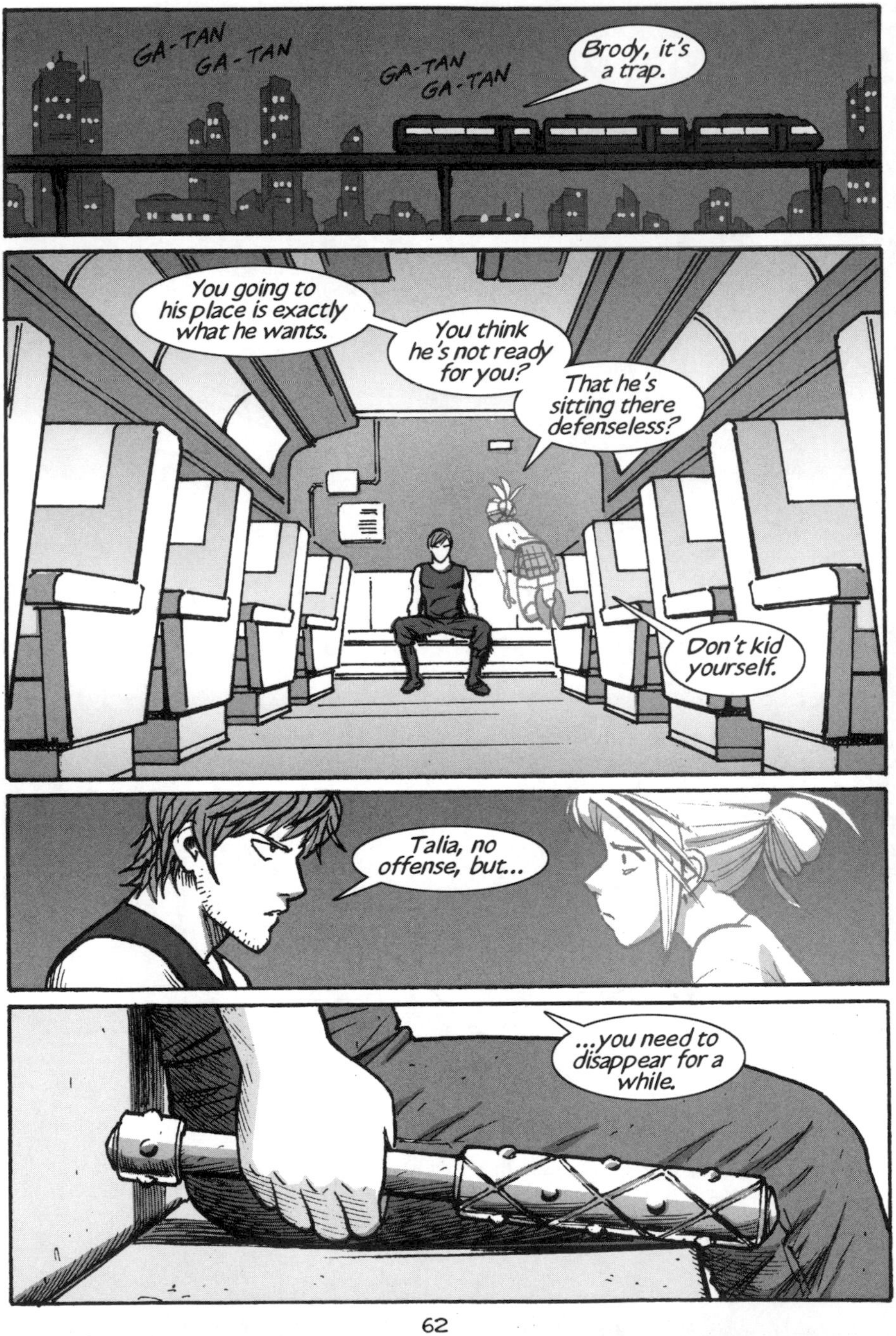
GA-TAN
GA-TAN
GA-TAN
GA-TAN
Brody, it's a trap.
You going to his place is exactly what he wants.
You think he's not ready for you?
That he's sitting there defenseless?
Don't kid yourself.
Talia, no offense, but...
...you need to disappear for a while.

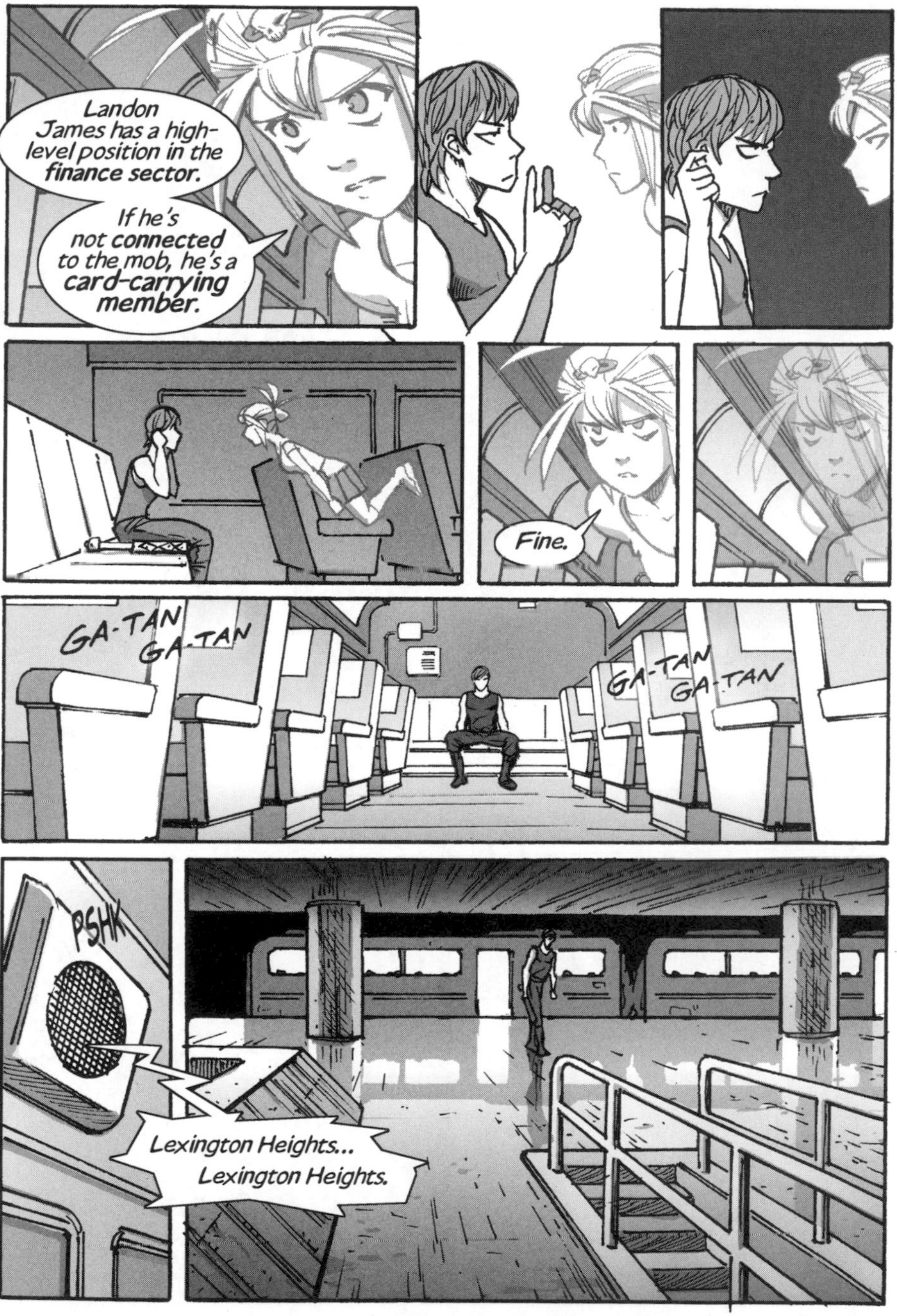
Landon James has a high-level position in the finance sector.
If he's not connected to the mob, he's a card-carrying member.
Fine.
GA-TAN GA-TAN
GA-TAN GA-TAN
PSHK
Lexington Heights... Lexington Heights.

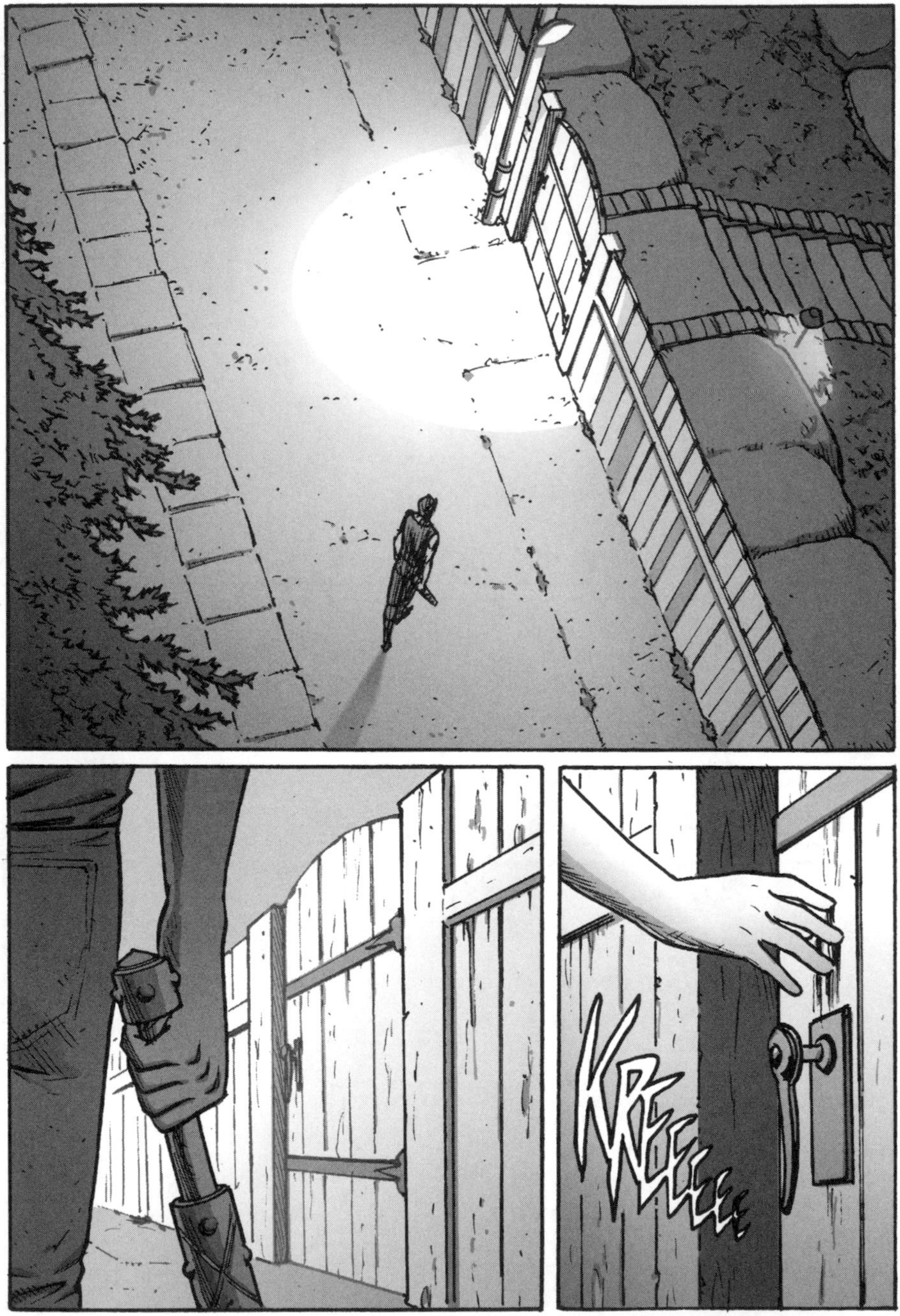
KREEEEEE

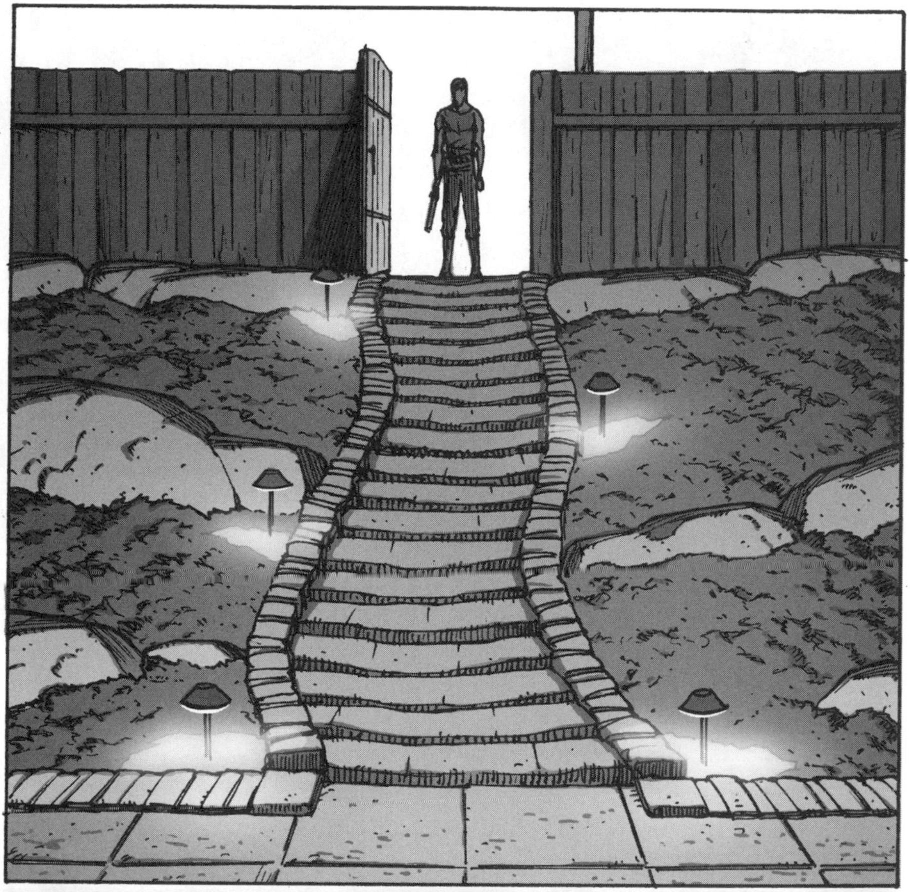
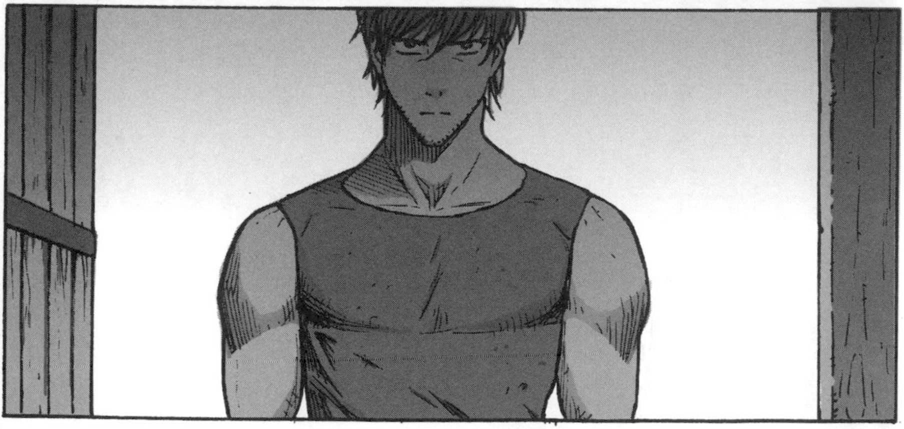

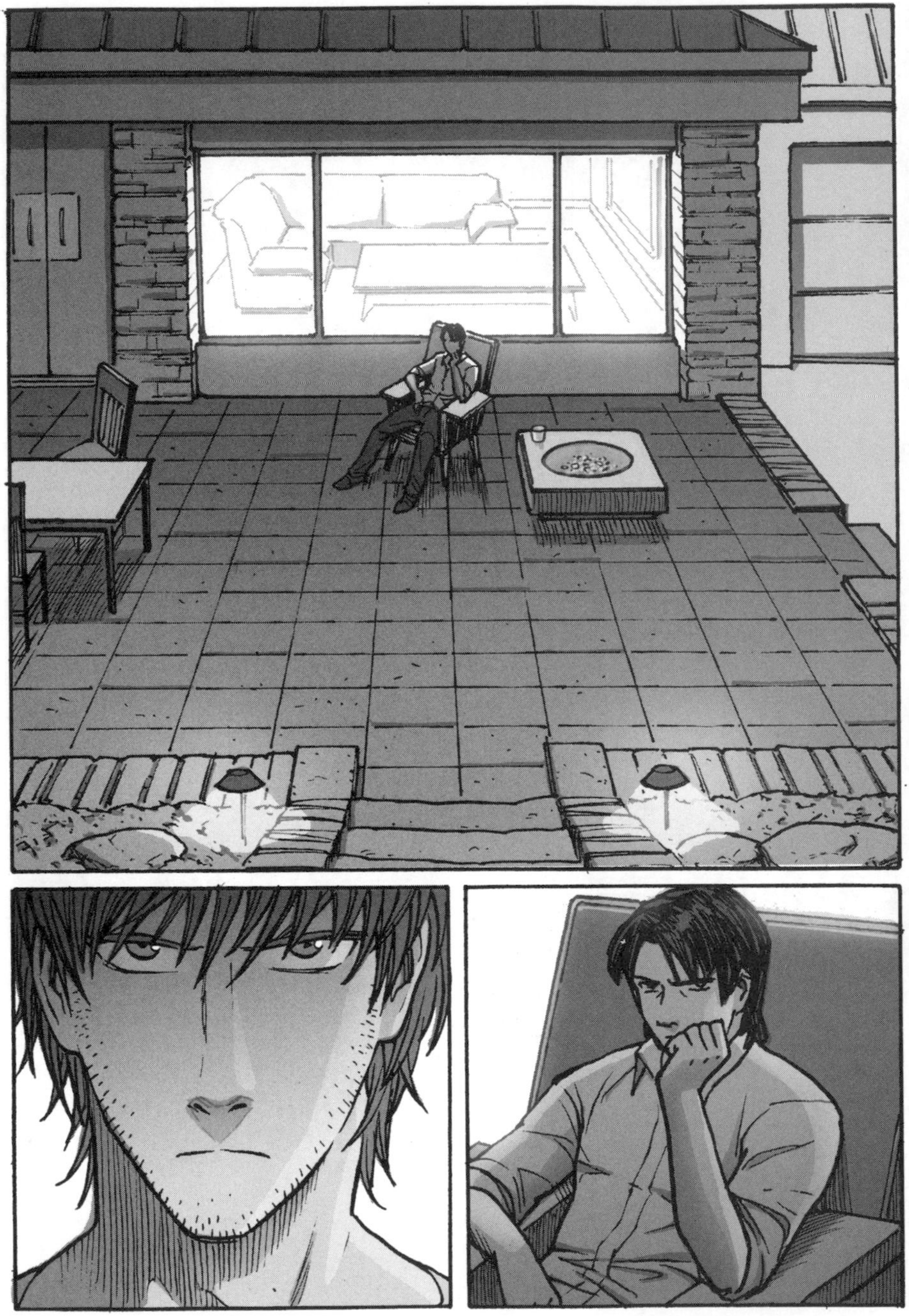

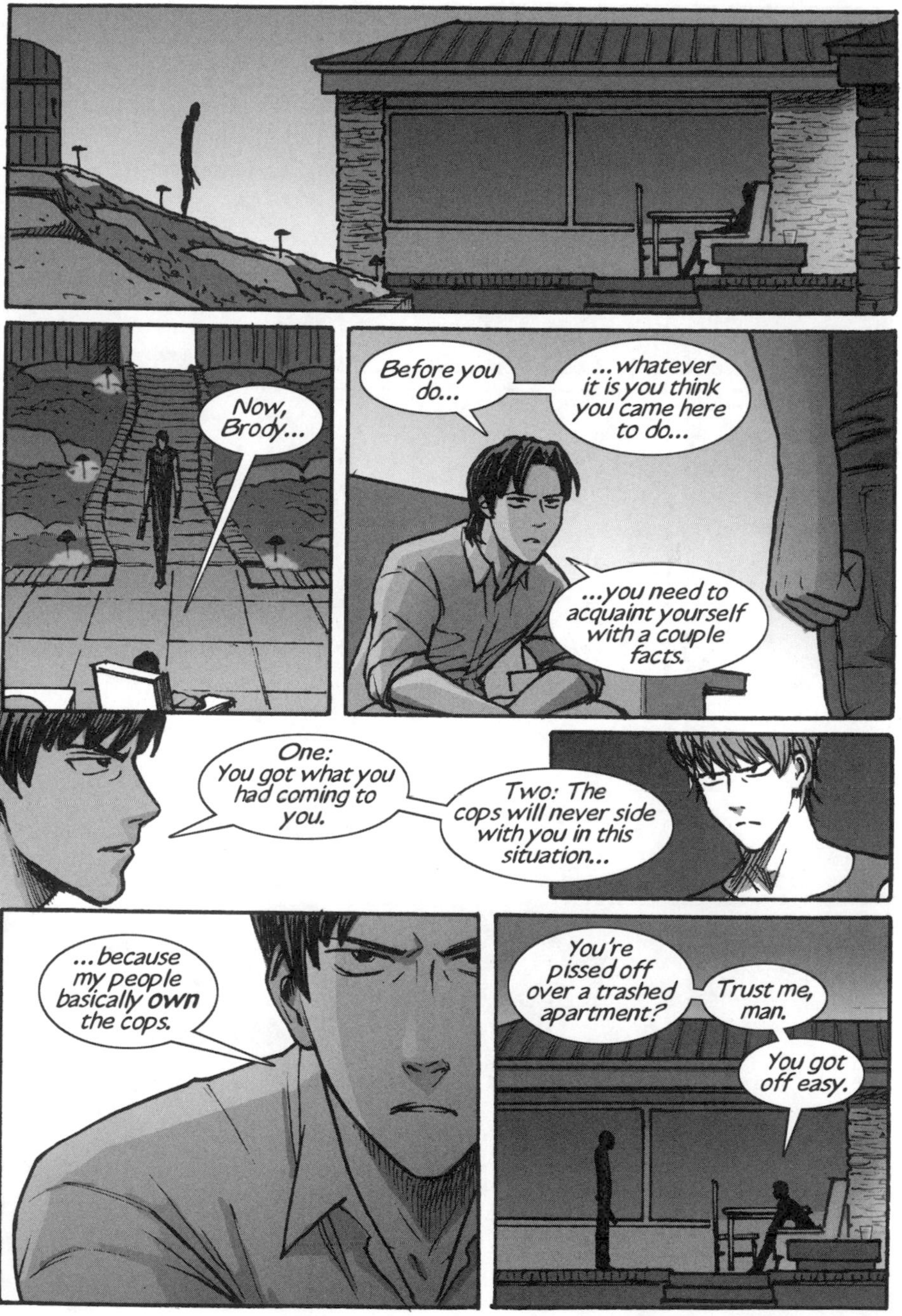

Now, Brody...
Before you do...
...whatever it is you think you came here to do...
...you need to acquaint yourself with a couple facts.
One: You got what you had coming to you.
Two: The cops will never side with you in this situation...
...because my people basically **own** the cops.
You're pissed off over a trashed apartment?
Trust me, man.
You got off easy.

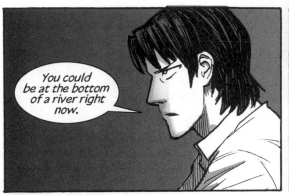

You could be at the bottom of a river right now.

I can make that happen.

Any time I want.

So before you make yet another colossally bad decision...

...I'd advise you to just go back home...

...pack up your stuff...

...and move out of town.

Forever.

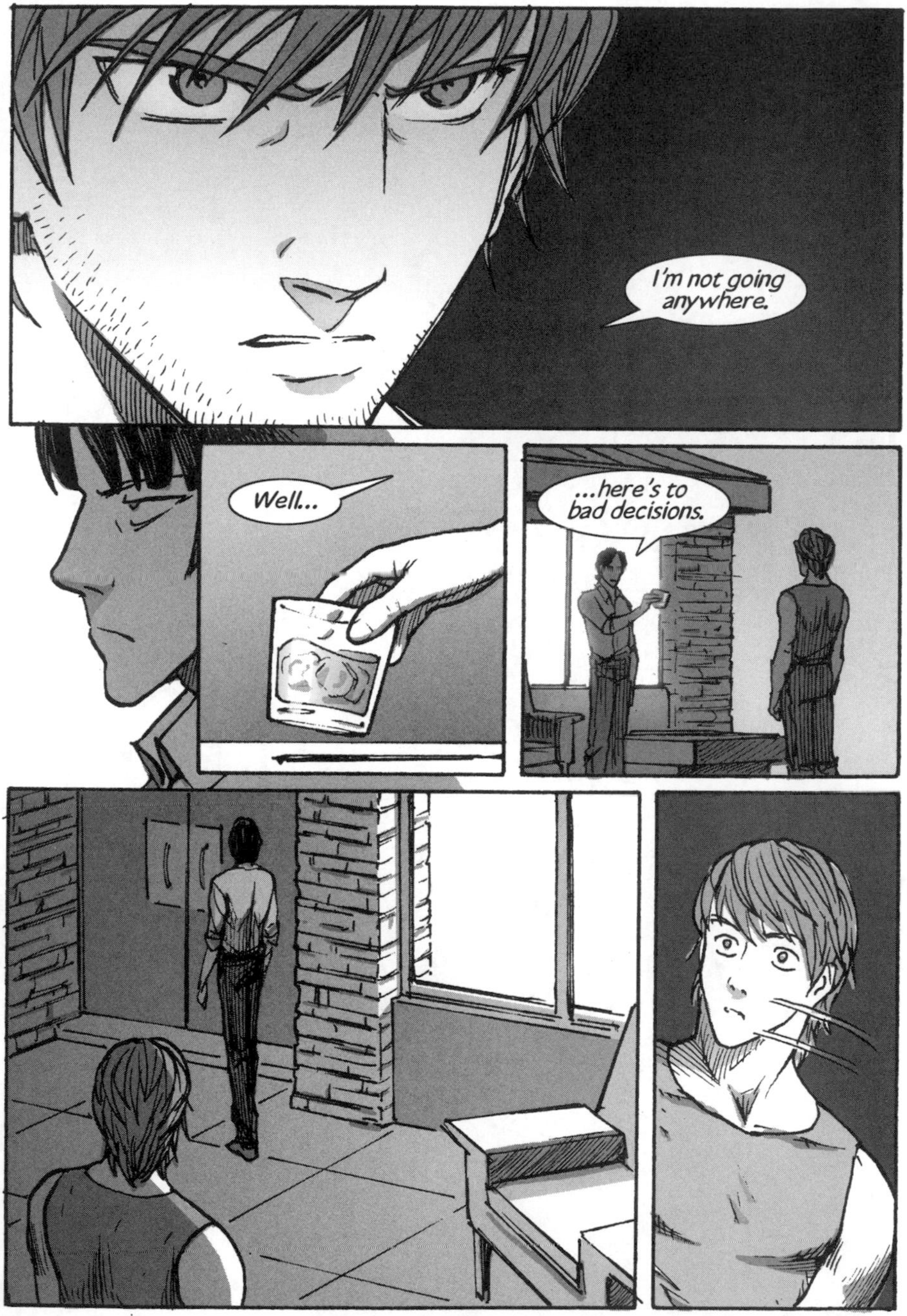
I'm not going anywhere.
Well...
...here's to bad decisions.

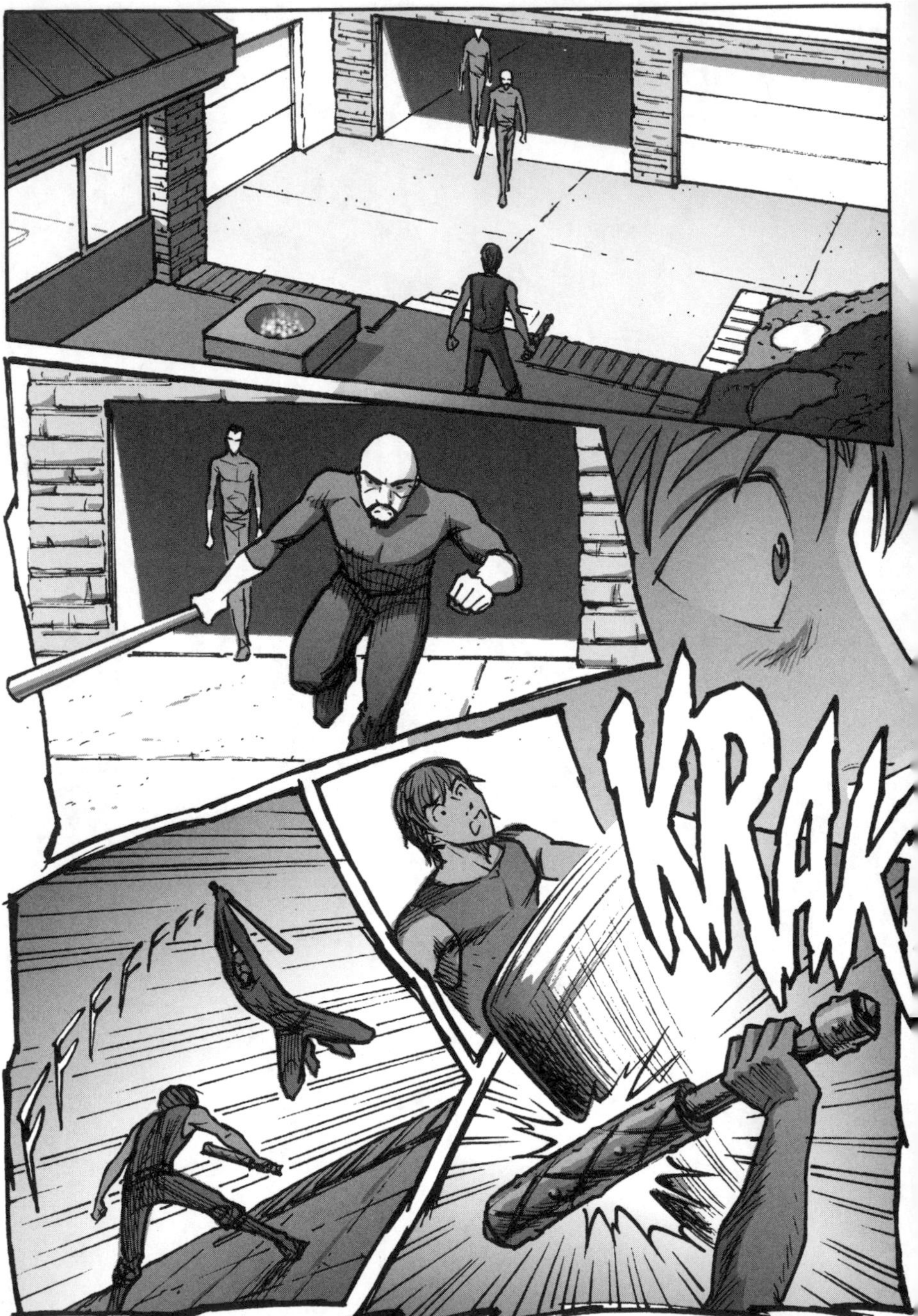
KRAK
FFFFFFFF

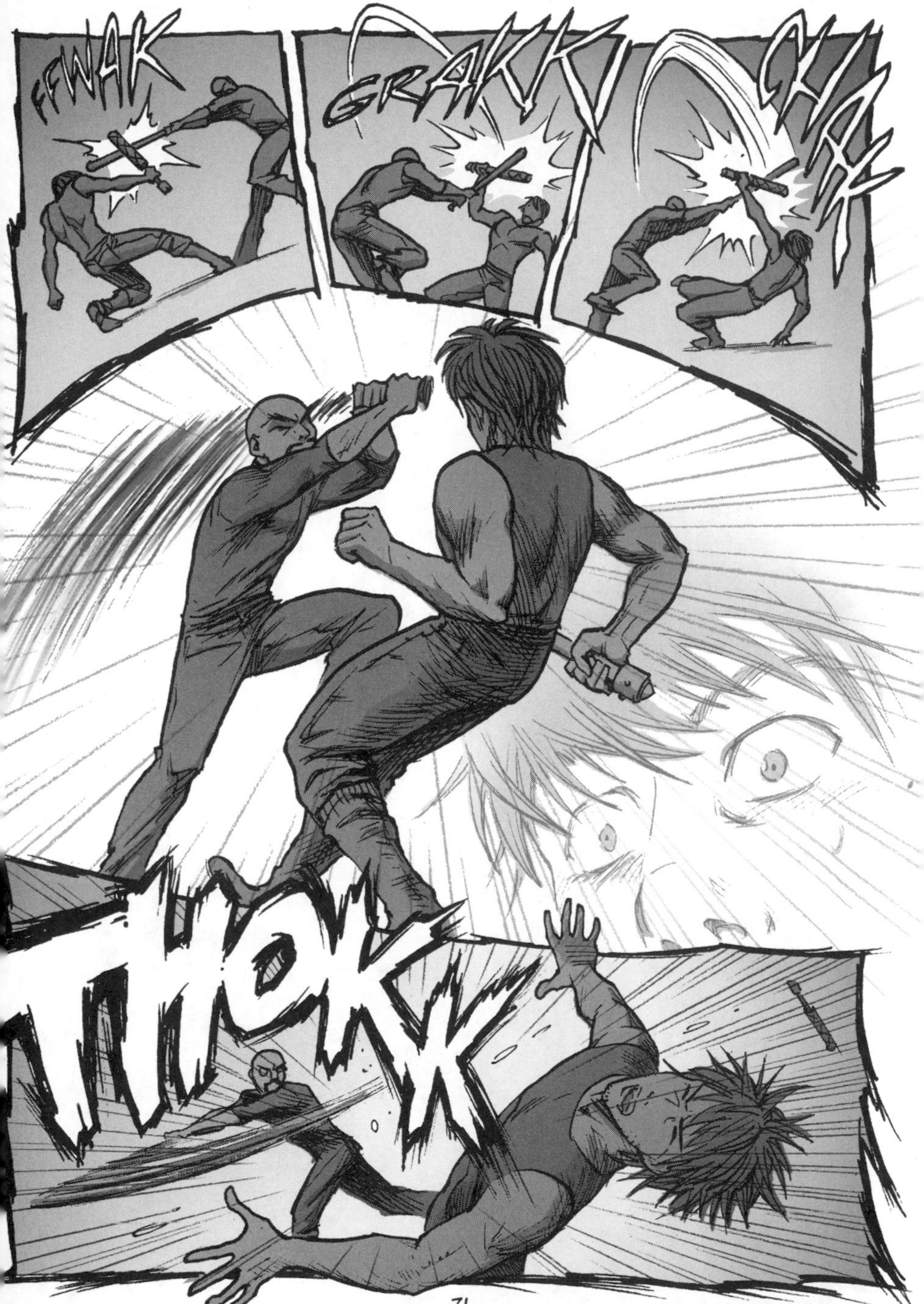
FFWAK
GRAKK
CHAK
THOK

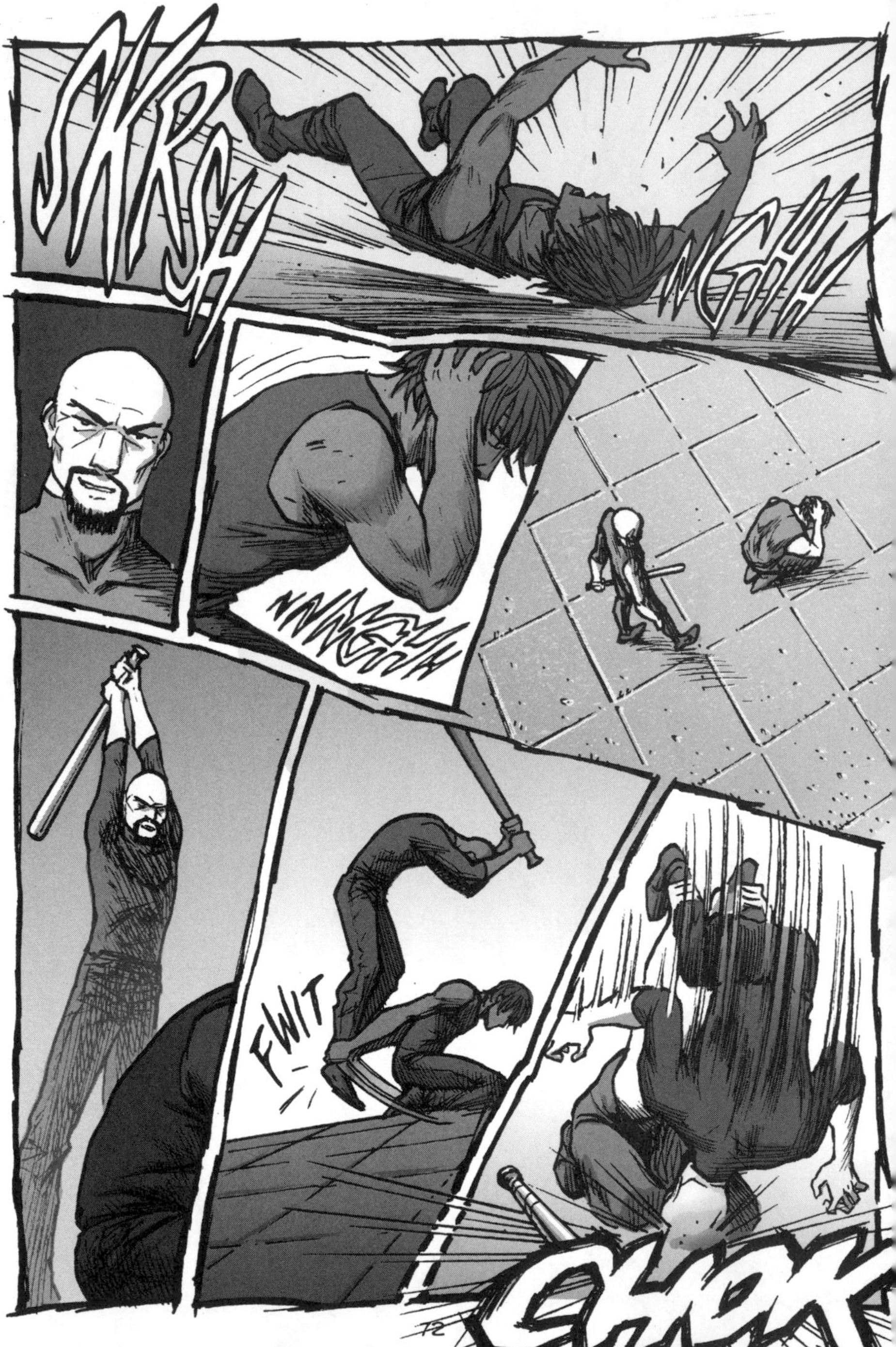
SKRSH
NGHH
NNNGHH
FWIT
CHOK

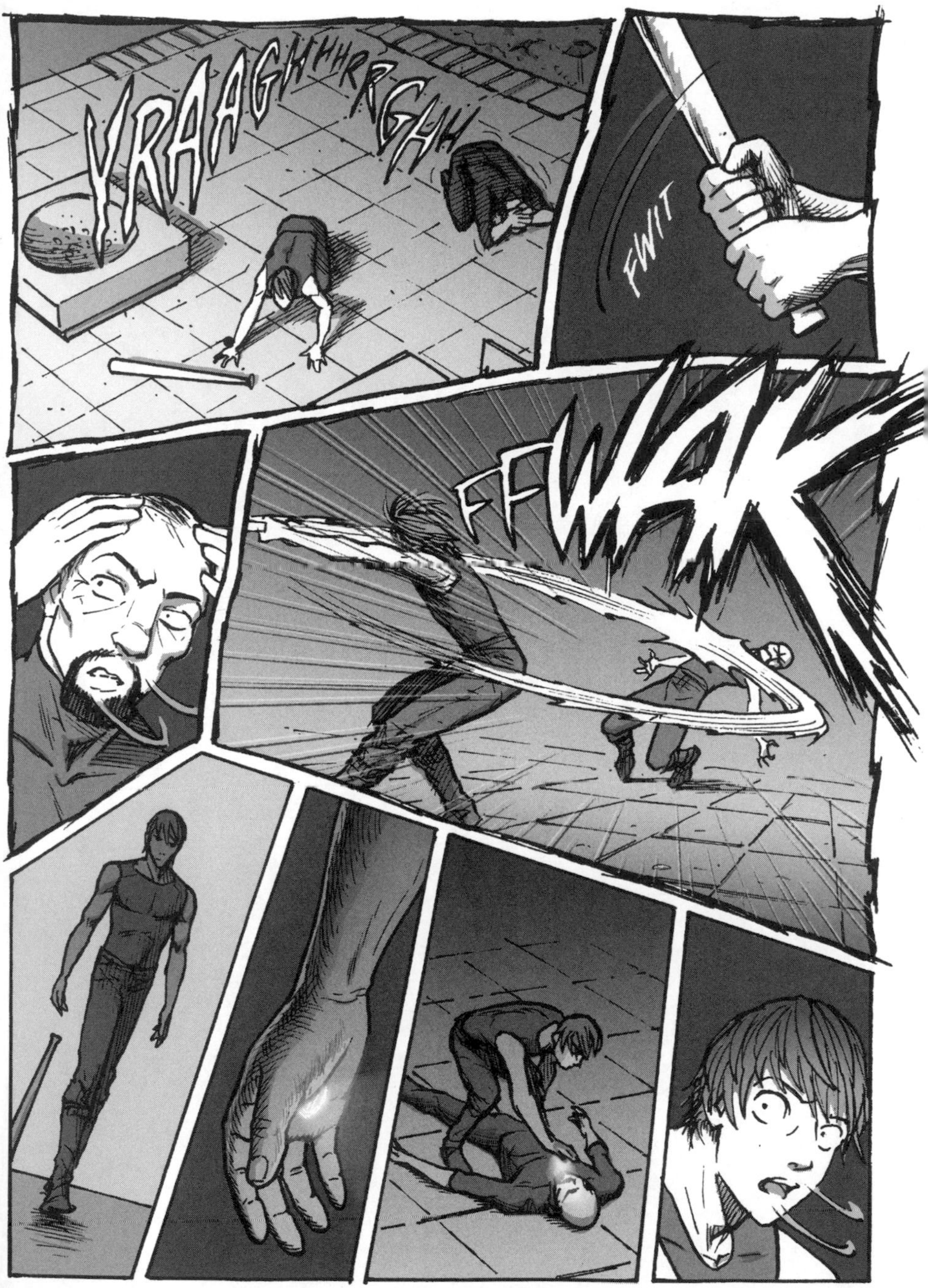
VRAAGHHRRGHH
FWIT
FFWAK

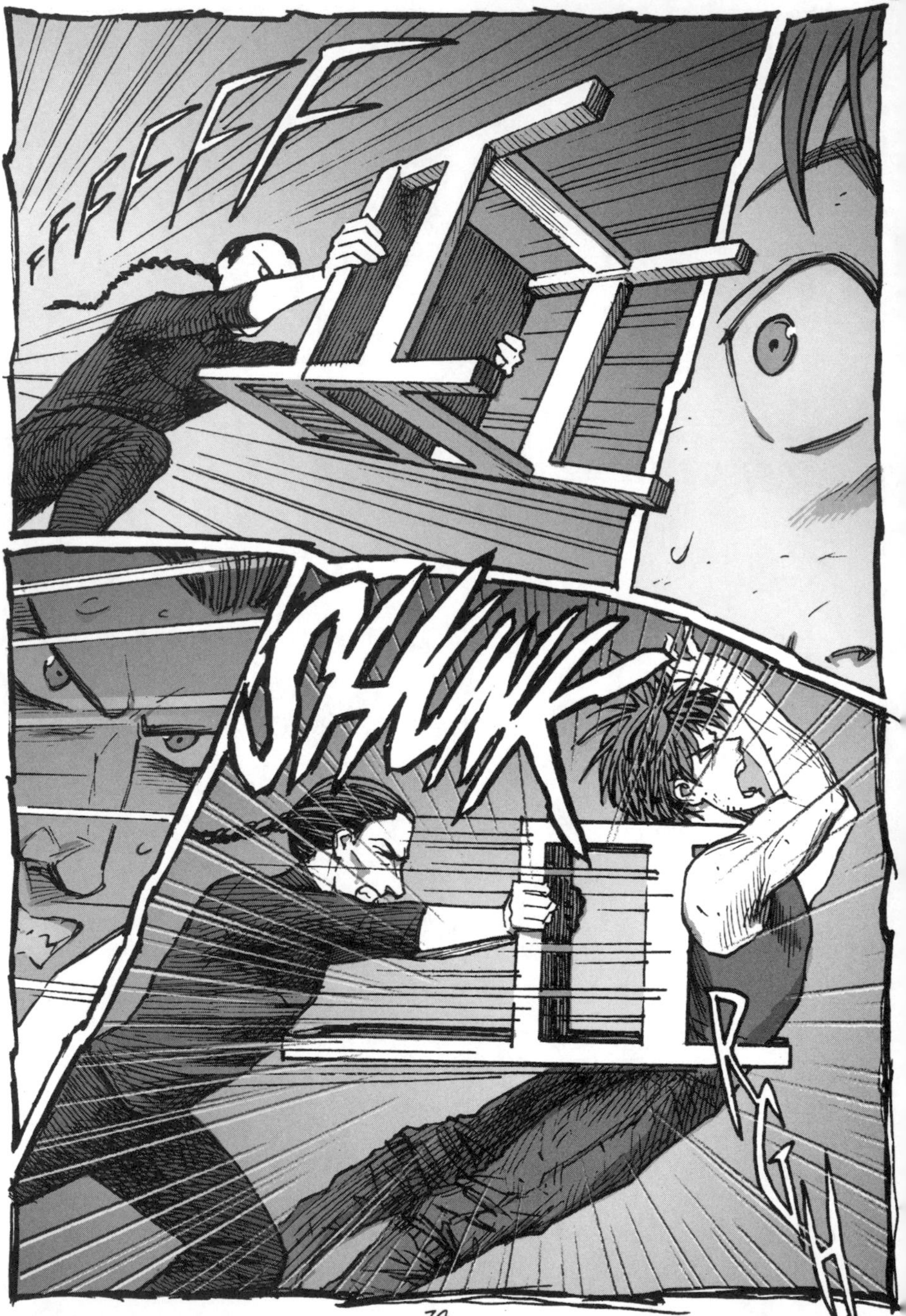
FFFFFFF
SHUNK
RCH

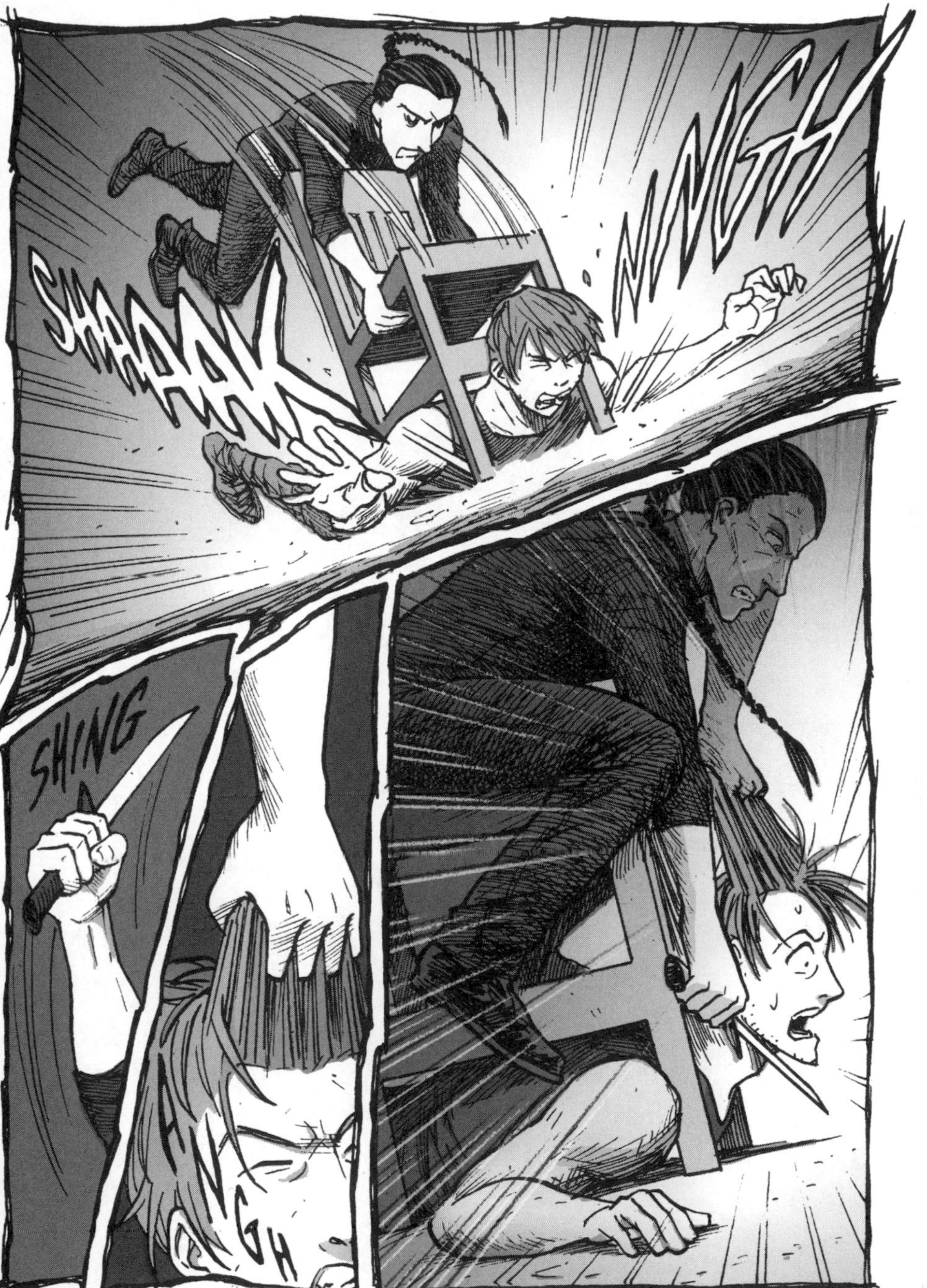
NNGH
SHING

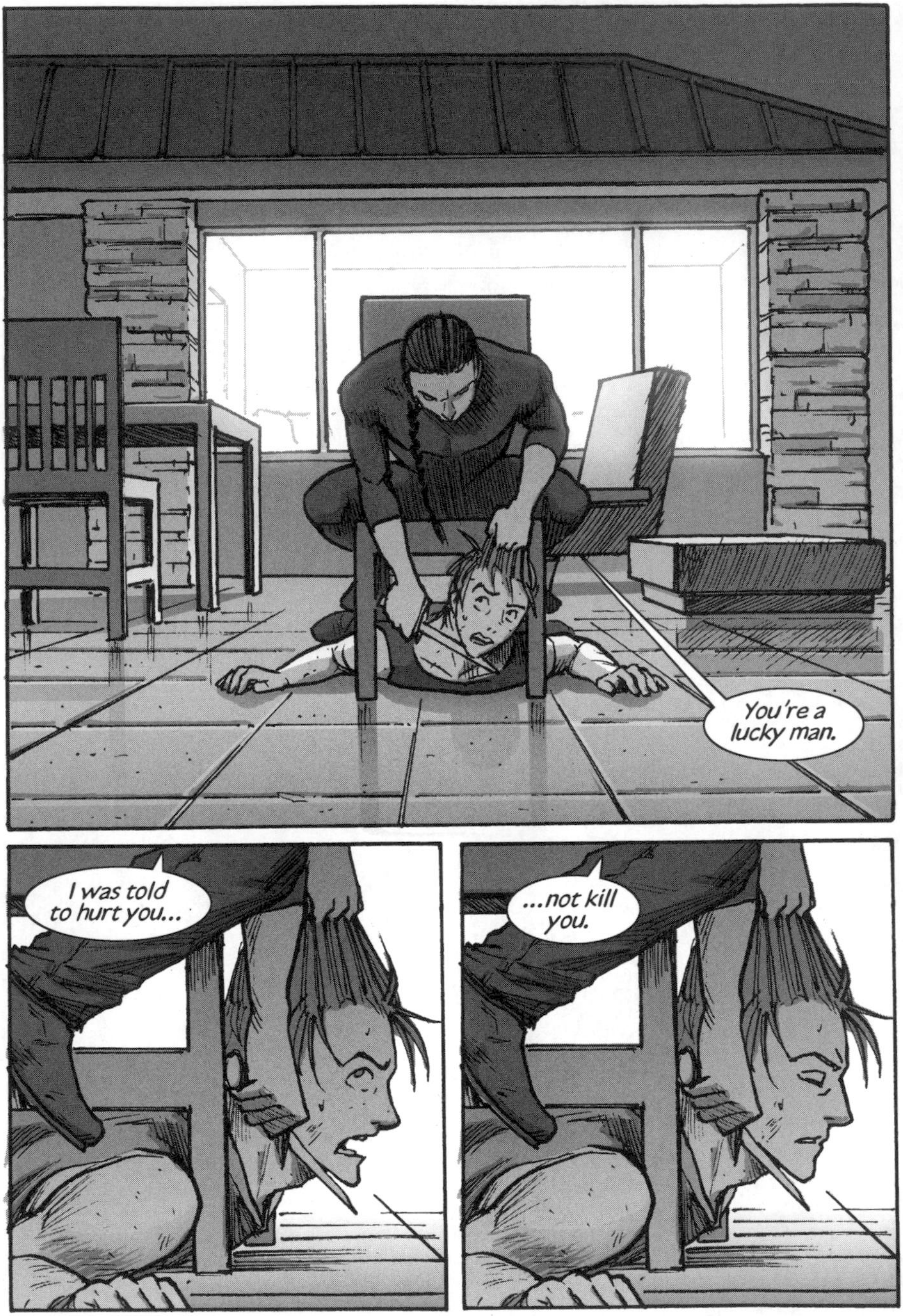
You're a lucky man.
I was told to hurt you...
...not kill you.

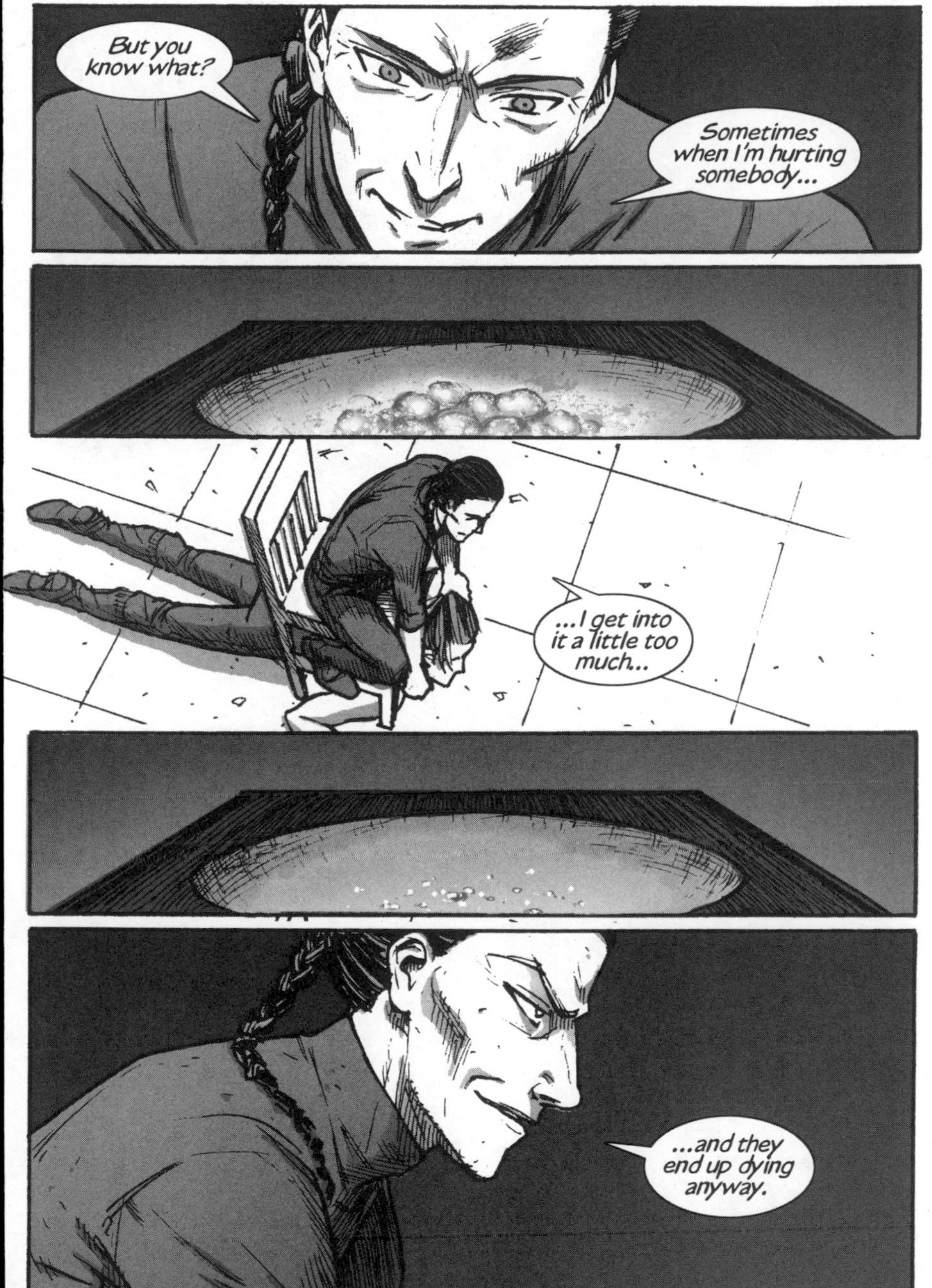
But you know what?
Sometimes when I'm hurting somebody...
...I get into it a little too much...
...and they end up dying anyway.

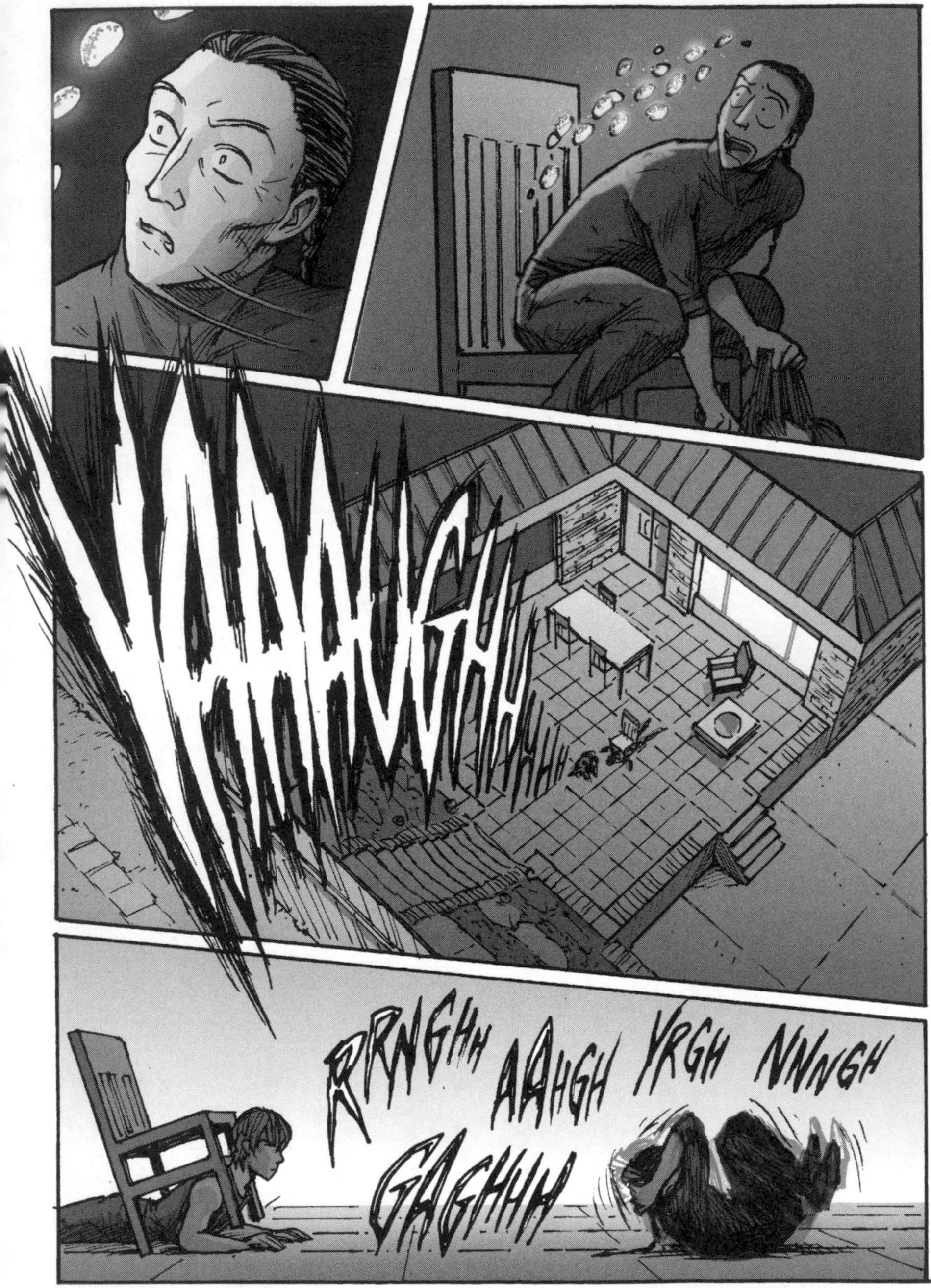
RRNGHH
AAHGH
YRGH
NNNGH
GAGHHH

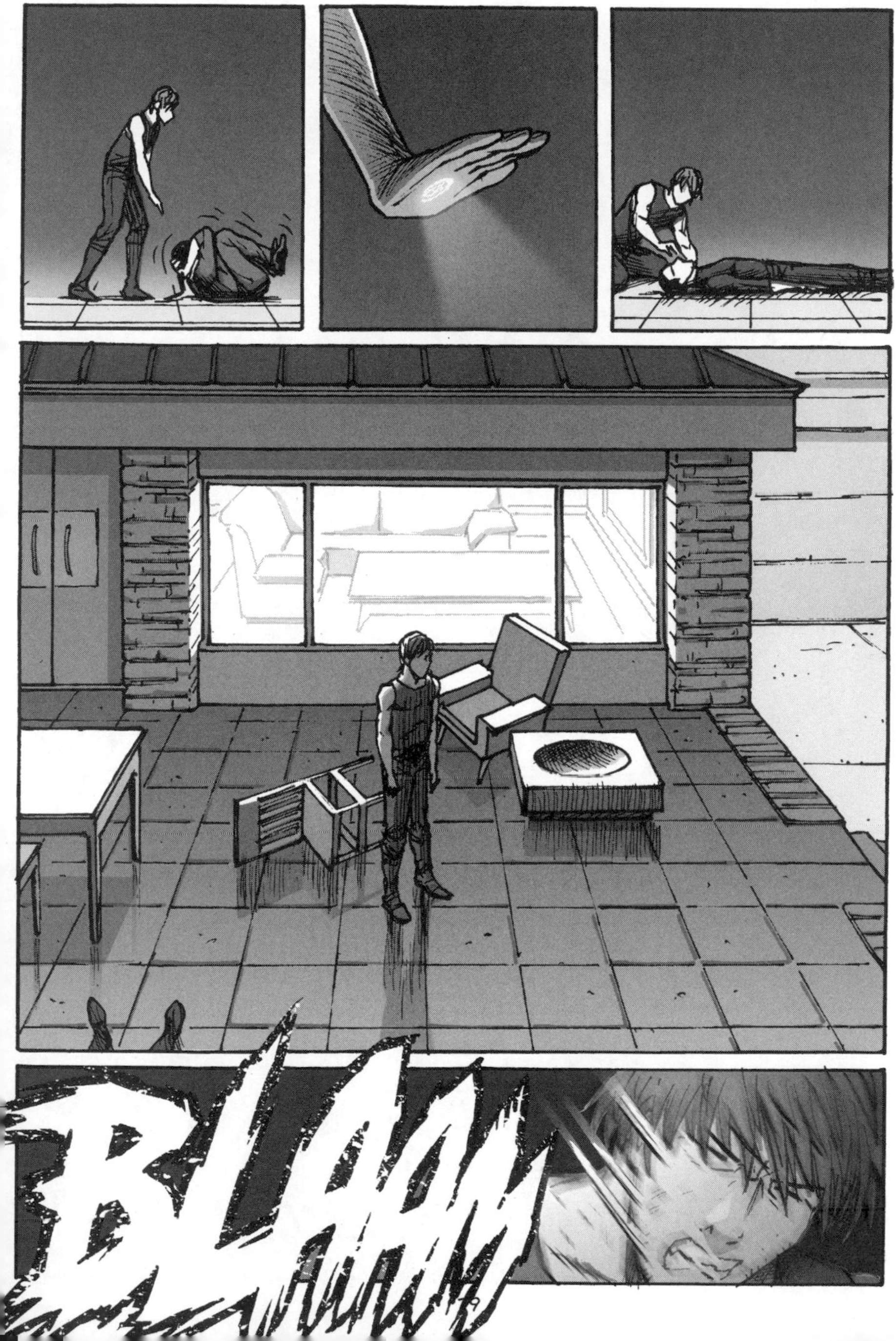
BLAAM

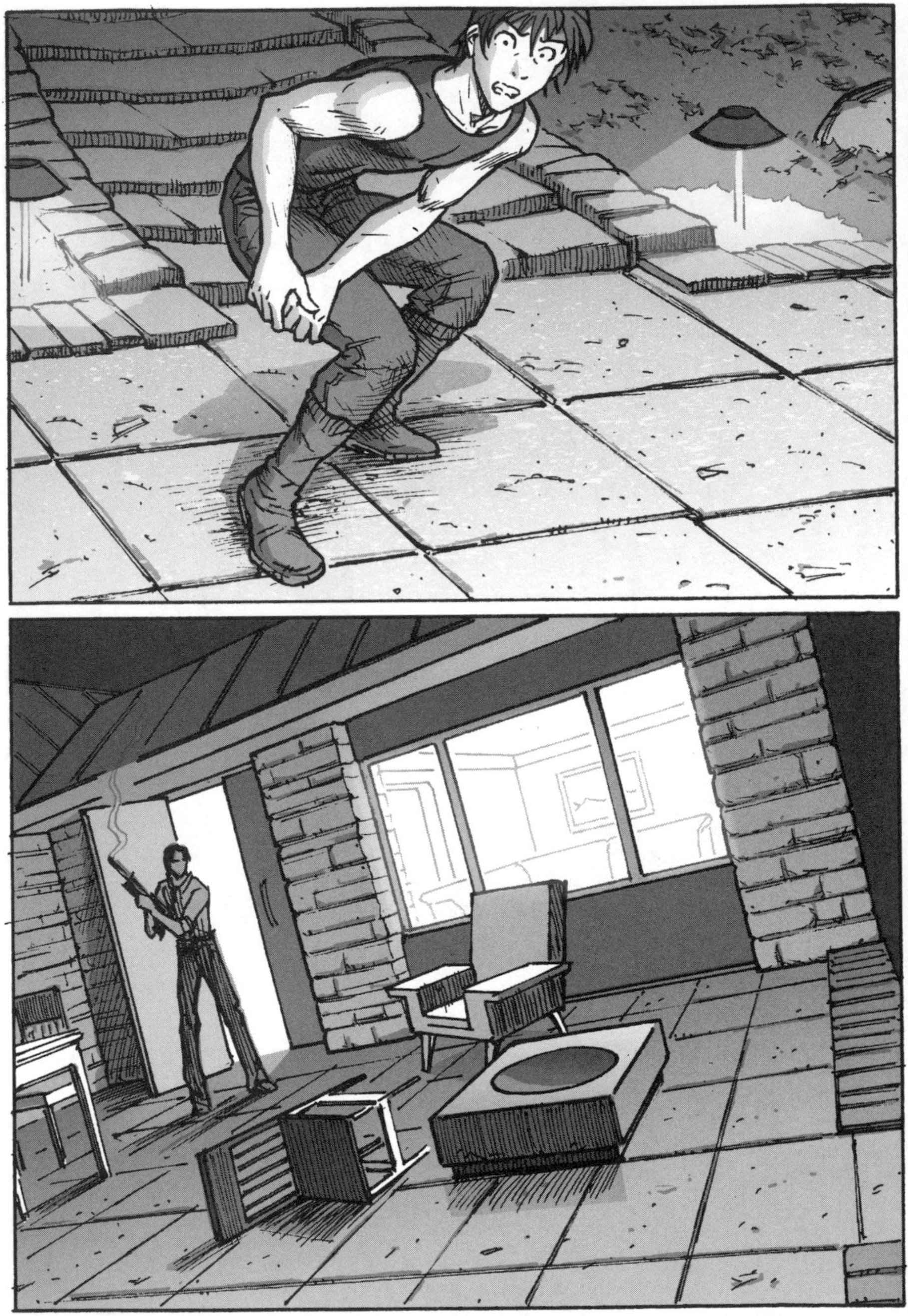

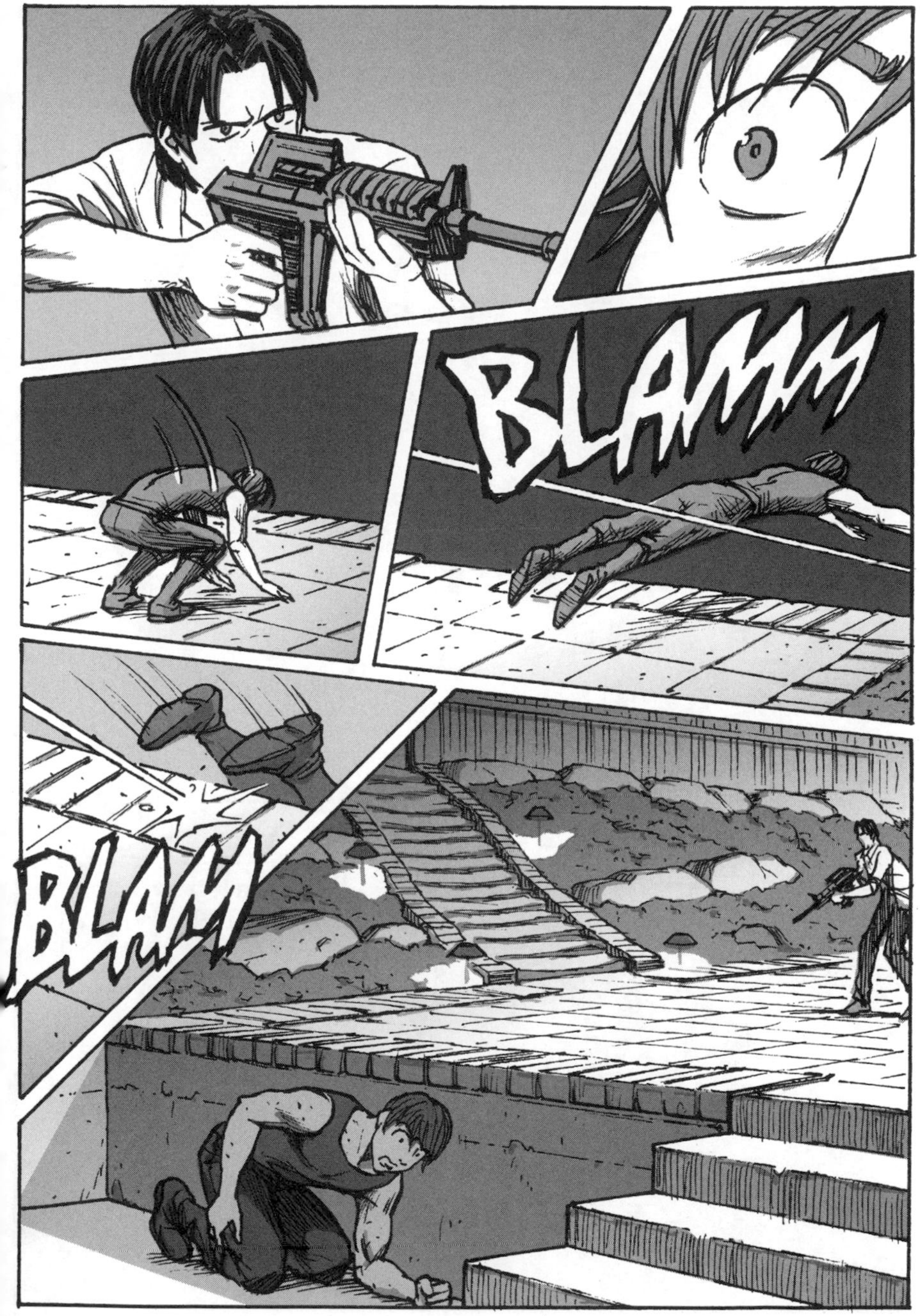
BLAMM
BLAM

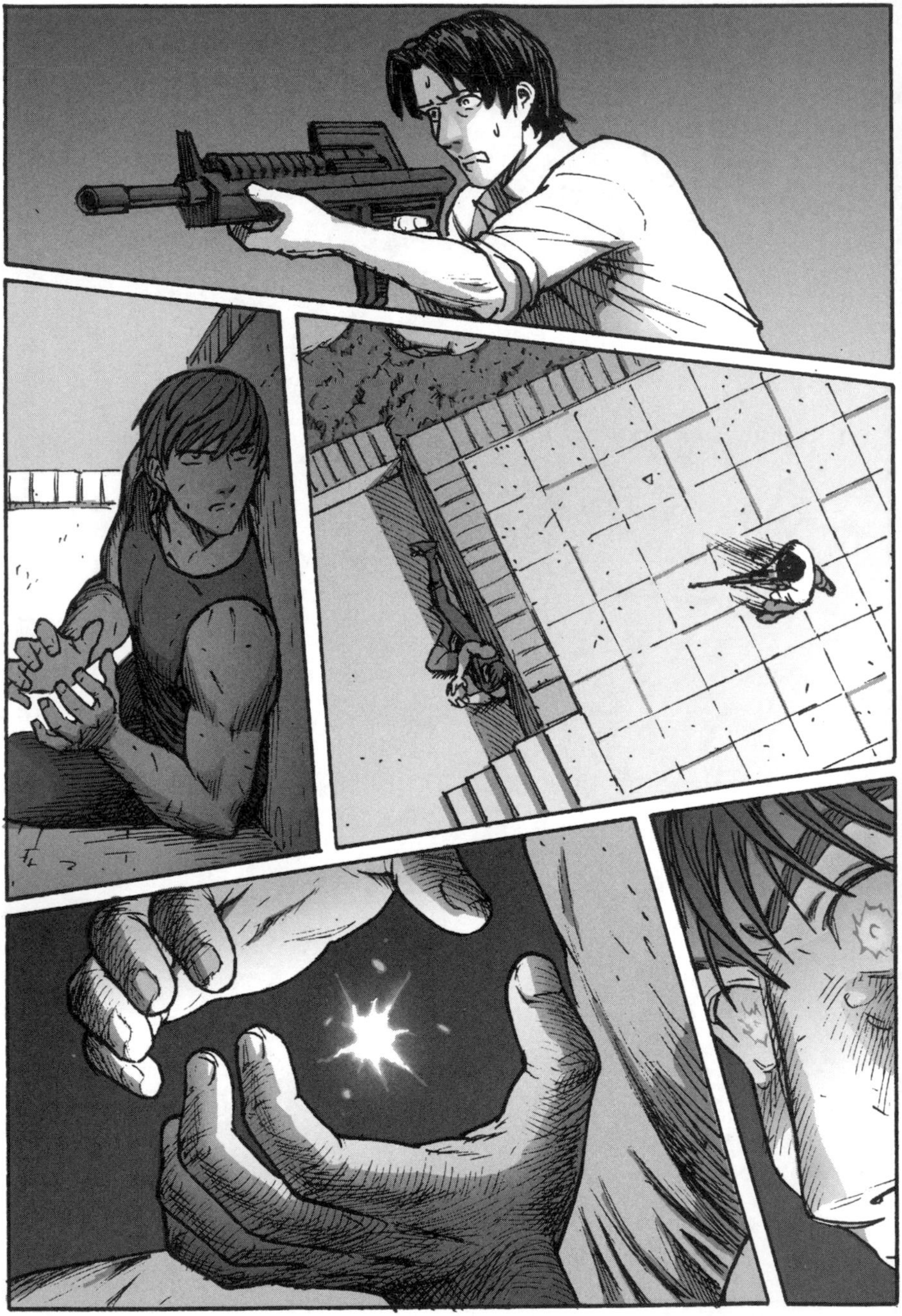

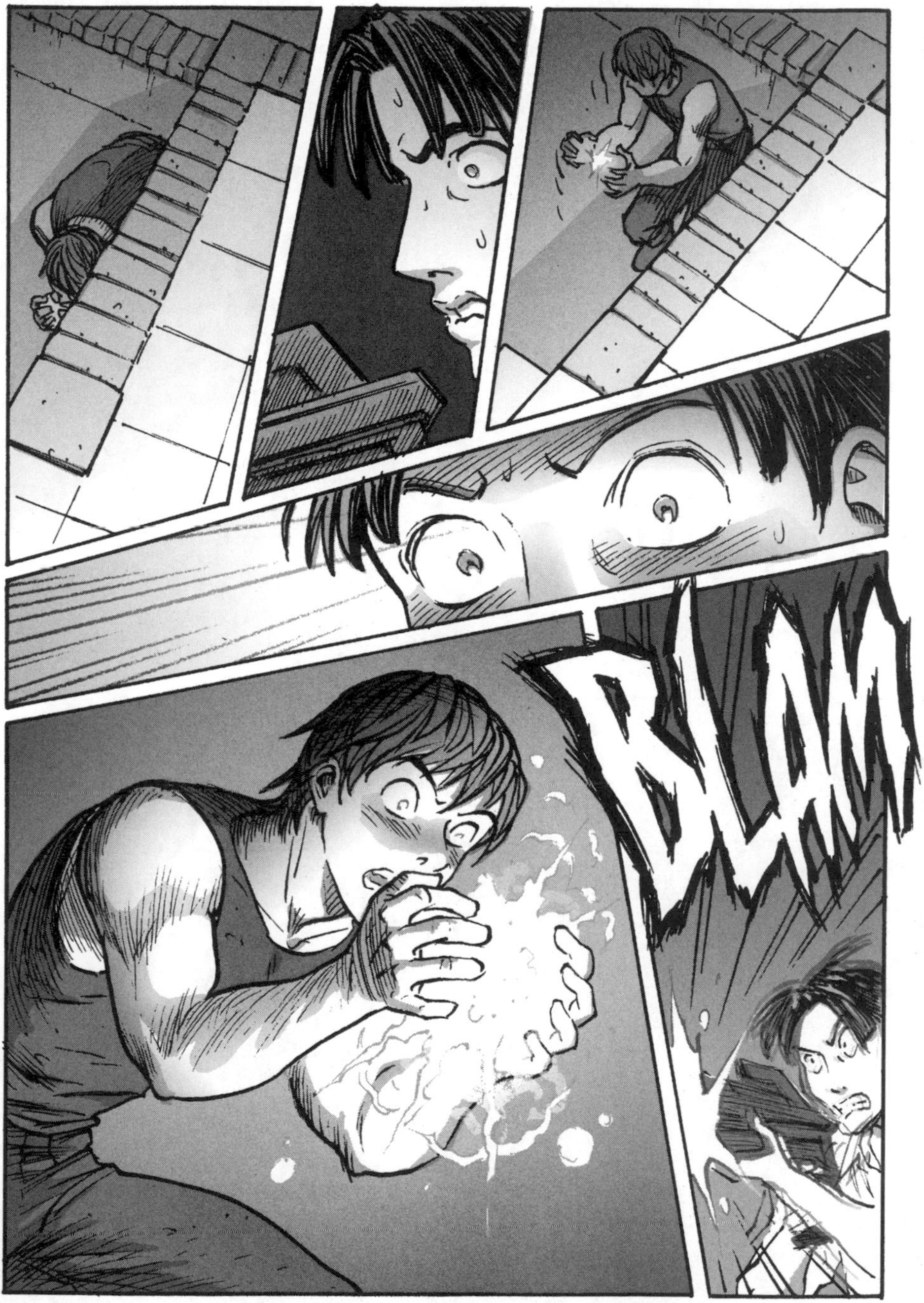
BLAM

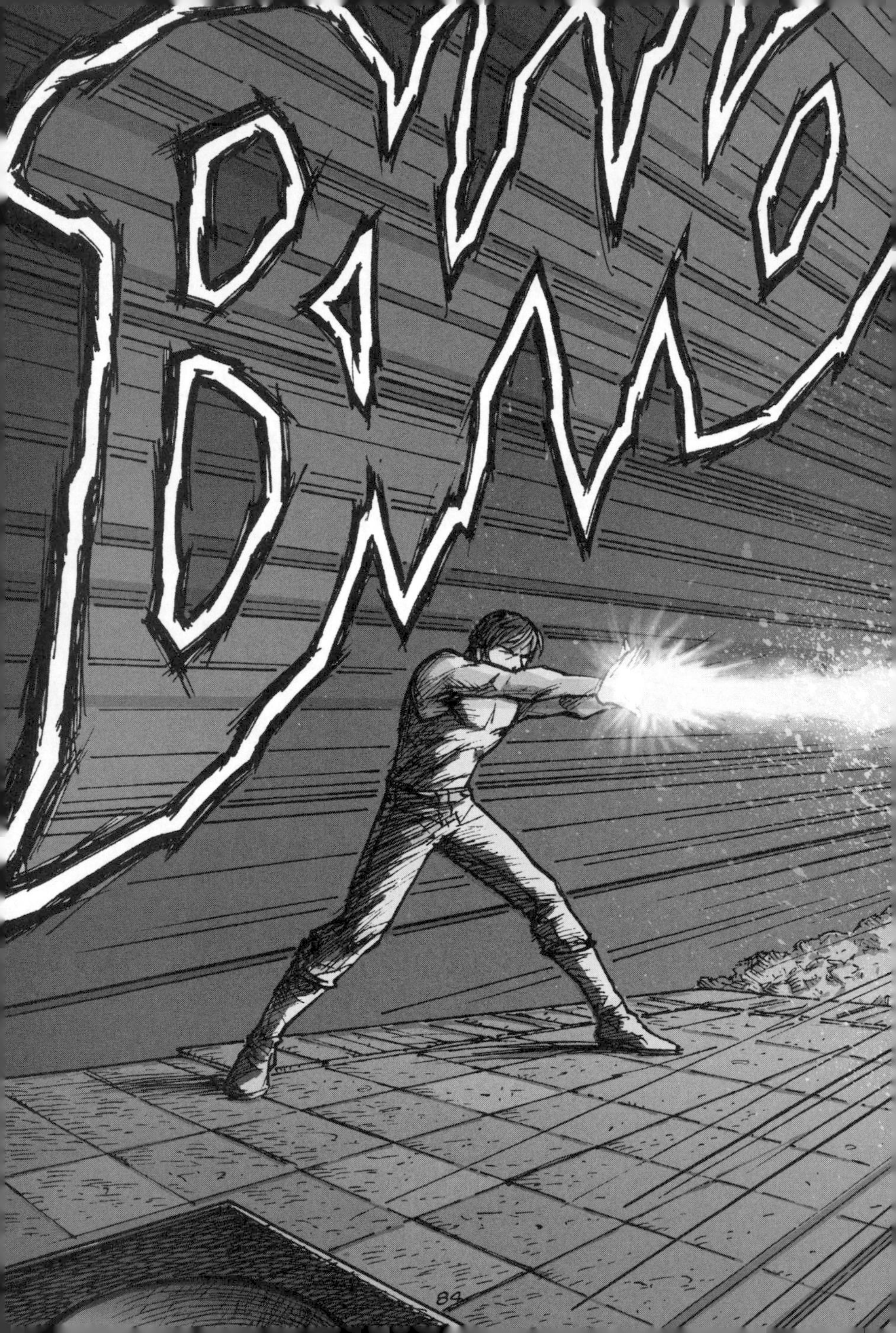

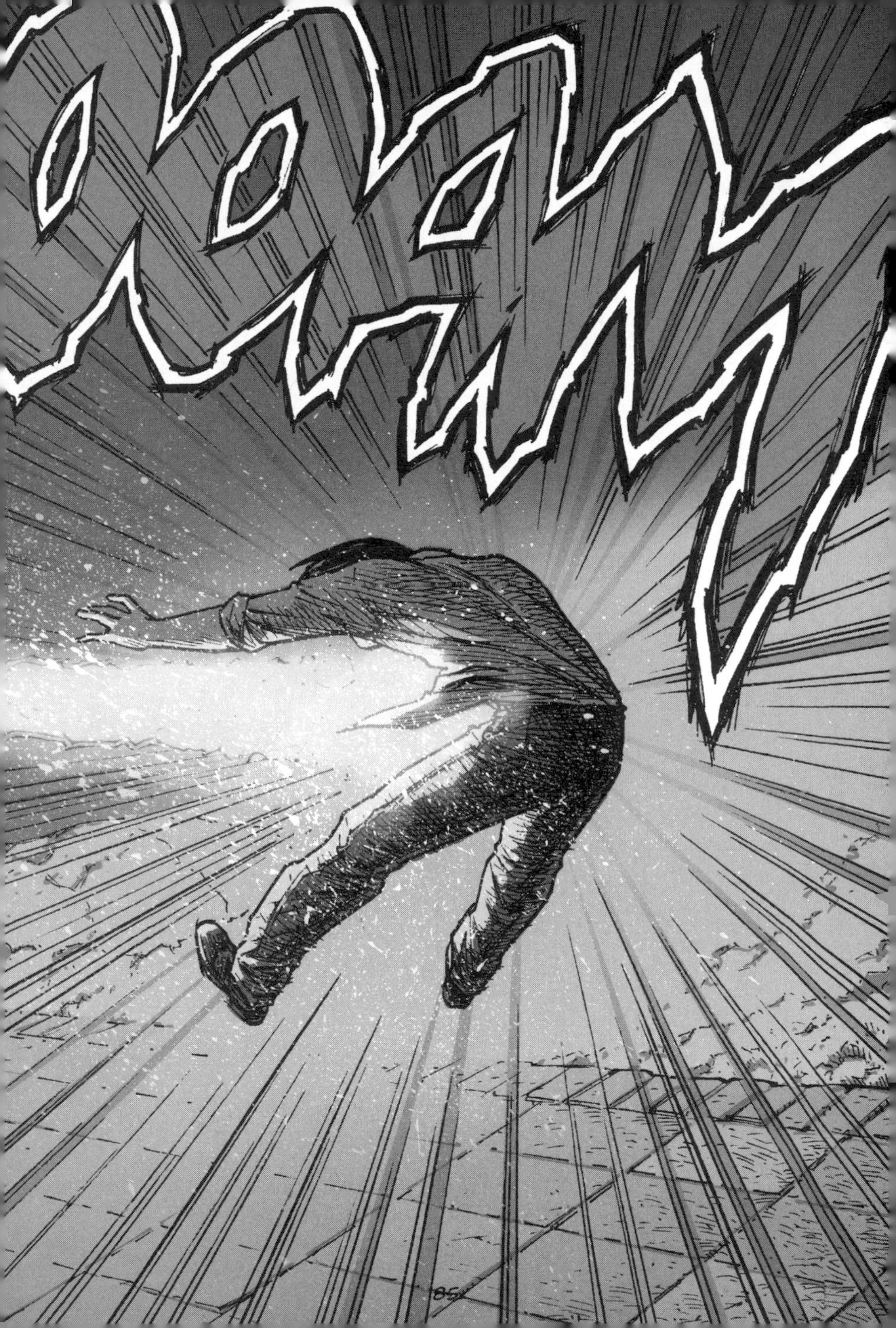

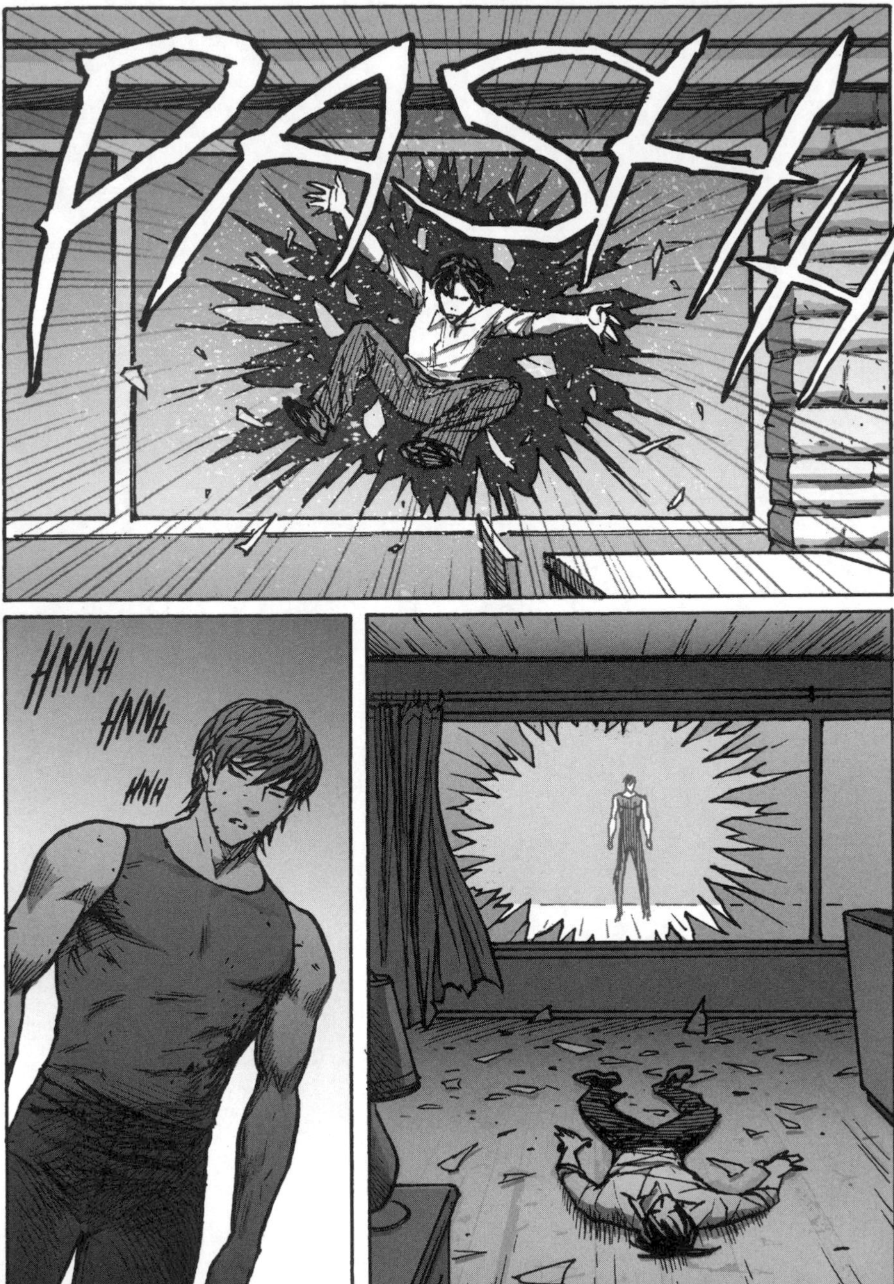
DASHH
HNNH
HNNH
HNH

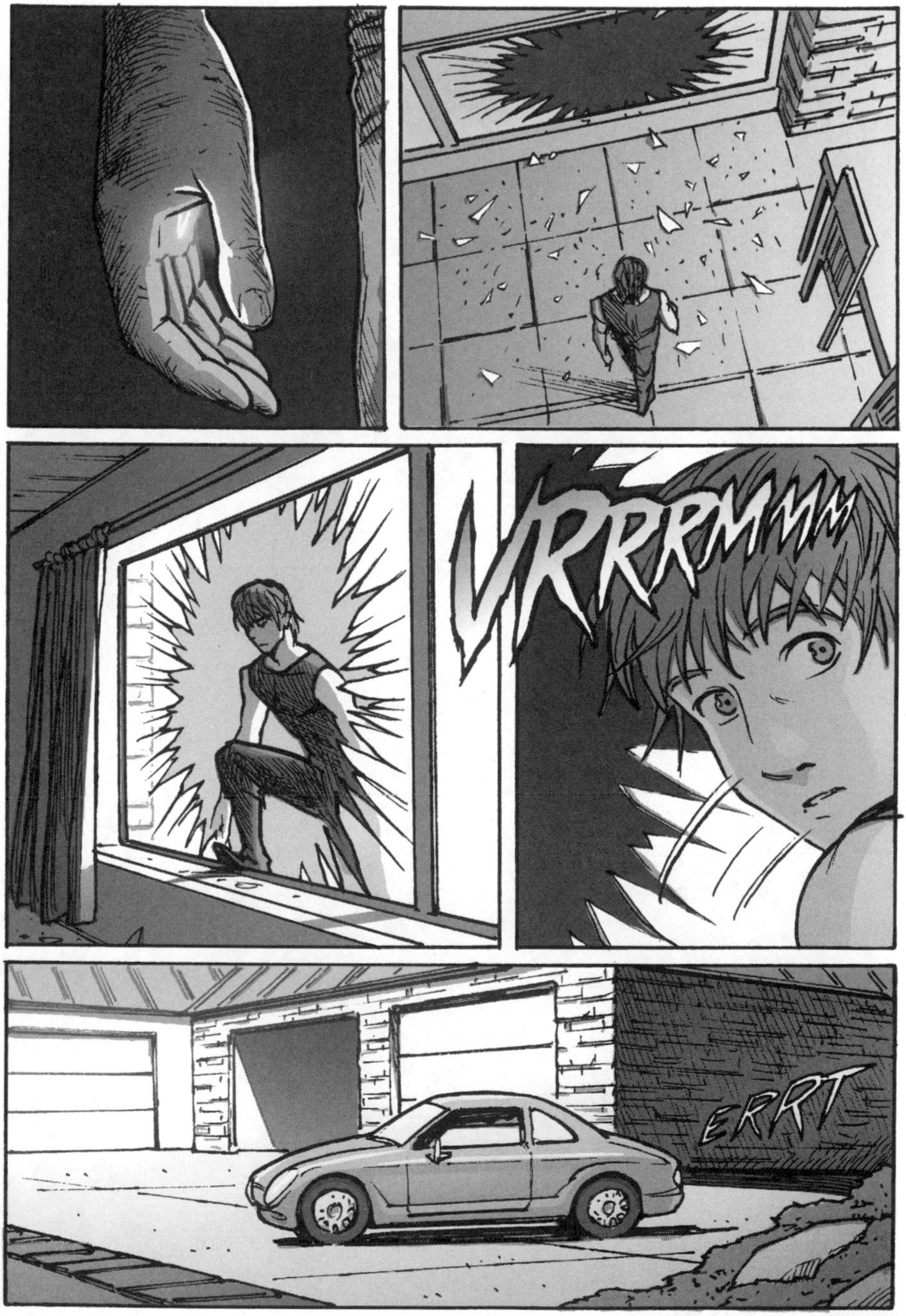
VRRRMMM
ERRT

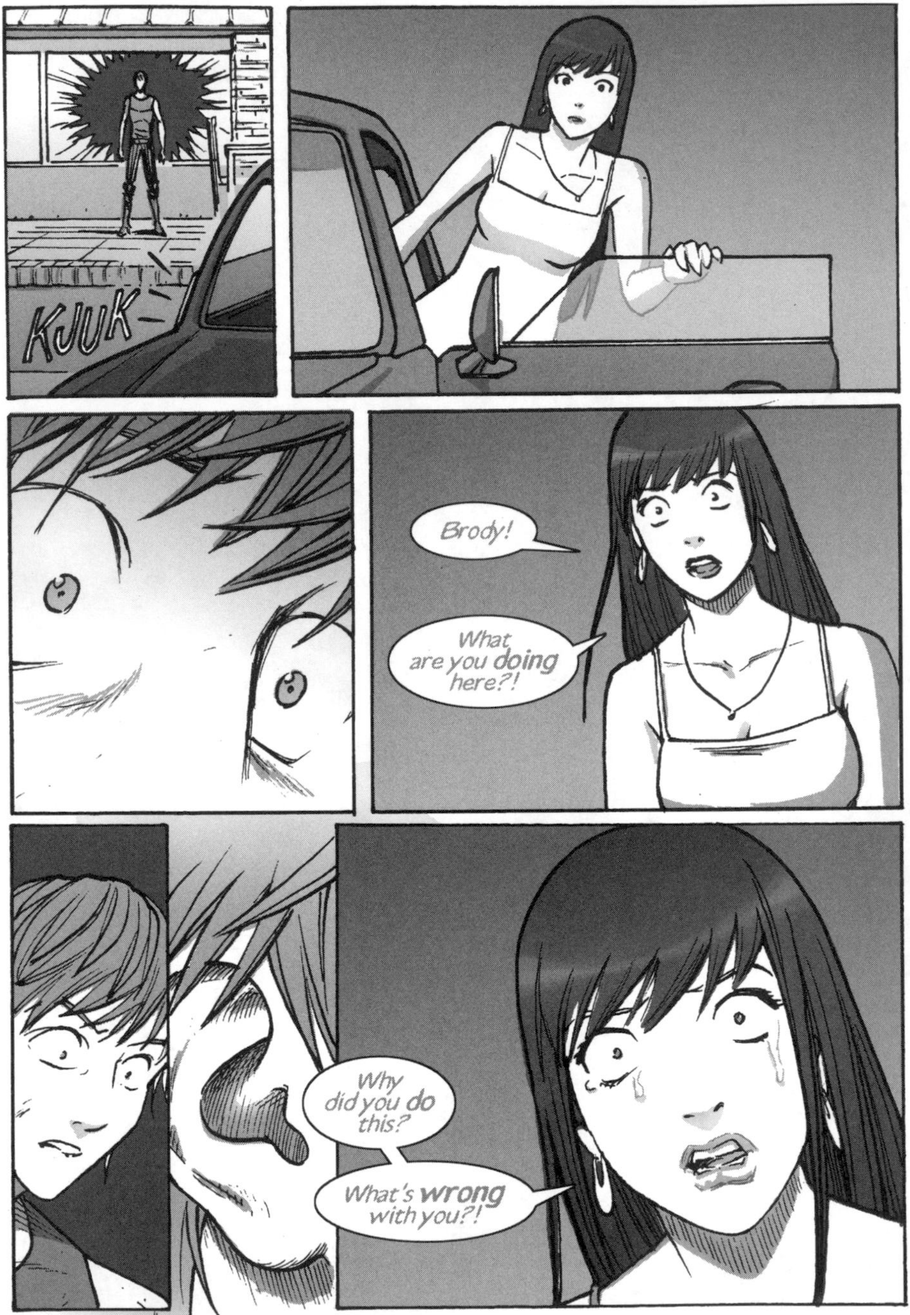
KJUK
Brody!
What are you doing here?!
Why did you do this?
What's wrong with you?!

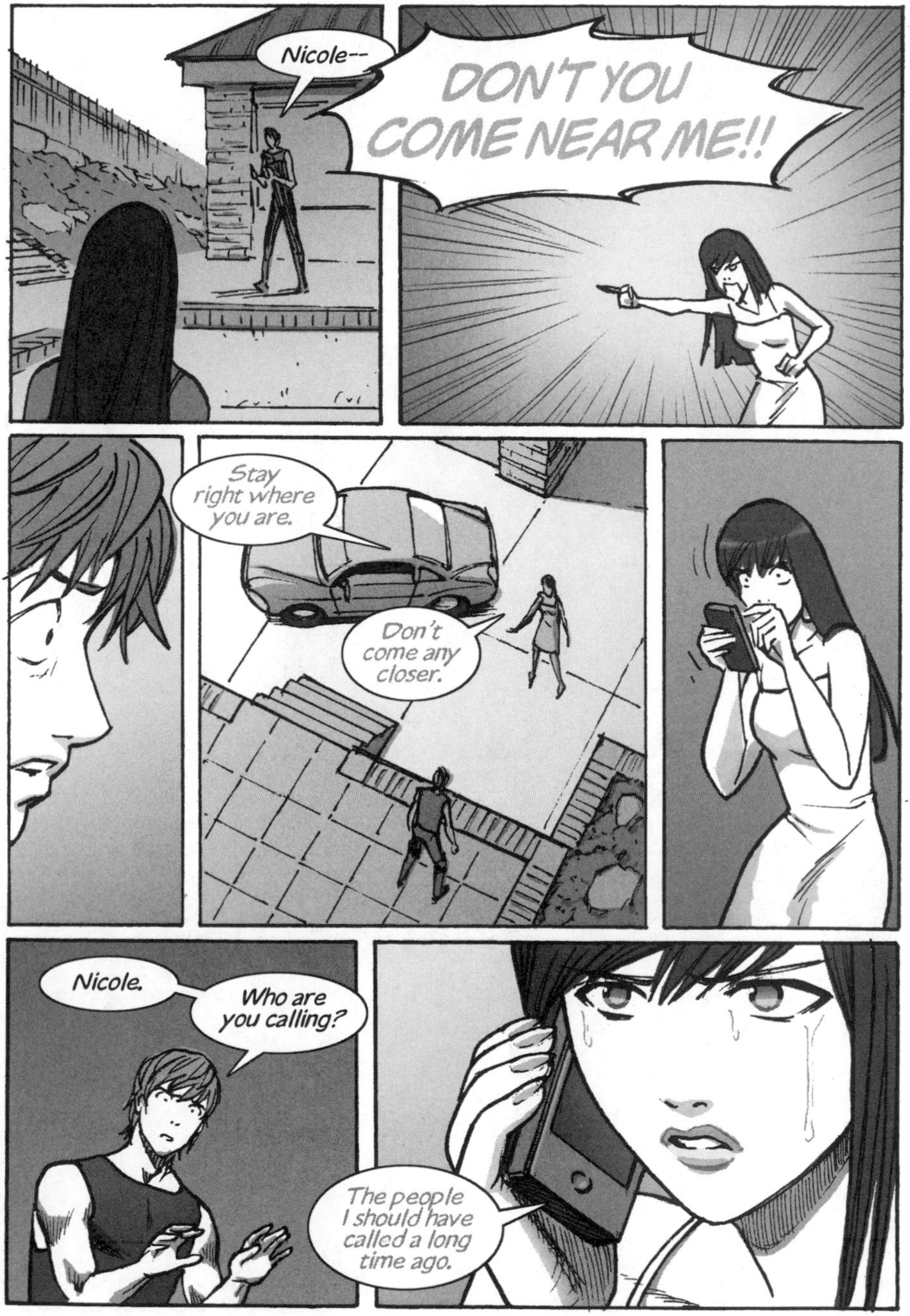
Nicole--
DON'T YOU COME NEAR ME!!
Stay right where you are.
Don't come any closer.
Nicole.
Who are you calling?
The people I should have called a long time ago.

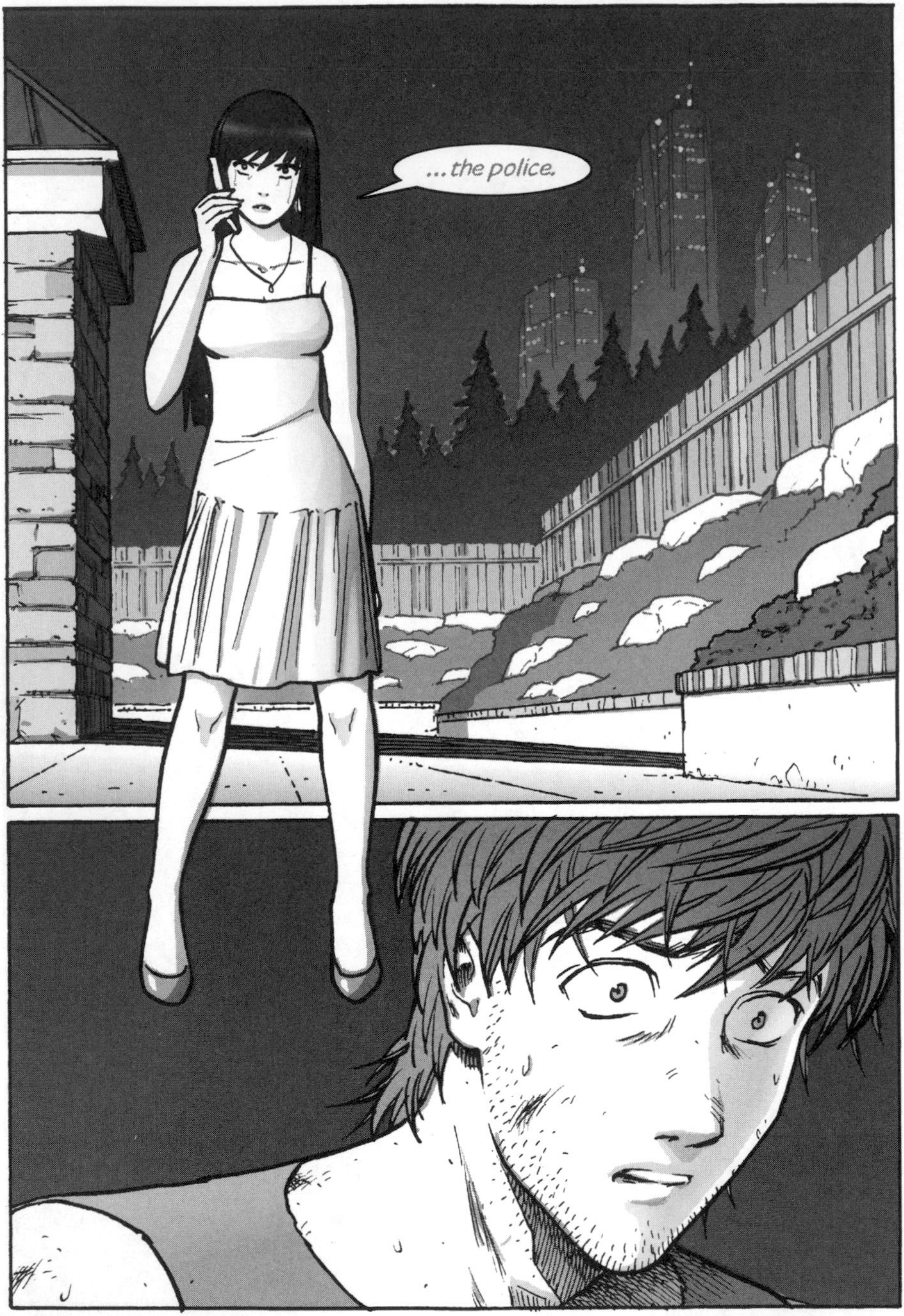
...the police.

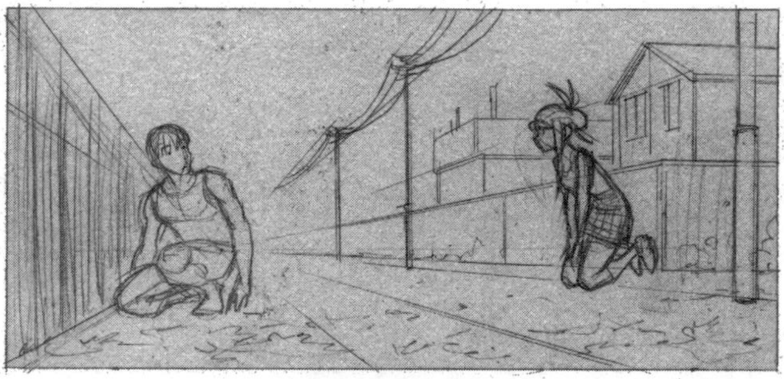

In my first draft of the book Landon's home was in a neighborhood with lots of other houses nearby. Giving things more thought, I felt it would be best to have him living in a wooded area, so that by going there Brody was truly in Landon's "kingdom," a place where Landon could do as he pleased without fear of any neighbors getting involved.

I knew I needed an interesting locale for the conversation between Brody and Gabe. I soon settled on placing it beside a canal, brightly lit to contrast the book's nighttime scenes. Initially a single-page illustration, I decided to expand it to help reestablish Brody's decaying urban world.

Sometimes you get a happy accident. When sketching out the guy who doesn't buy Brody's story I first wanted a neutral facial expression but got this creepy, dead eyed stare instead. I liked it so much I chose to stay very close to it in the final line art.

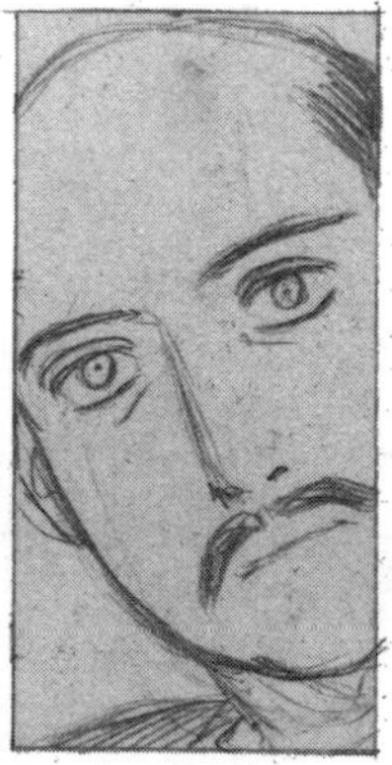

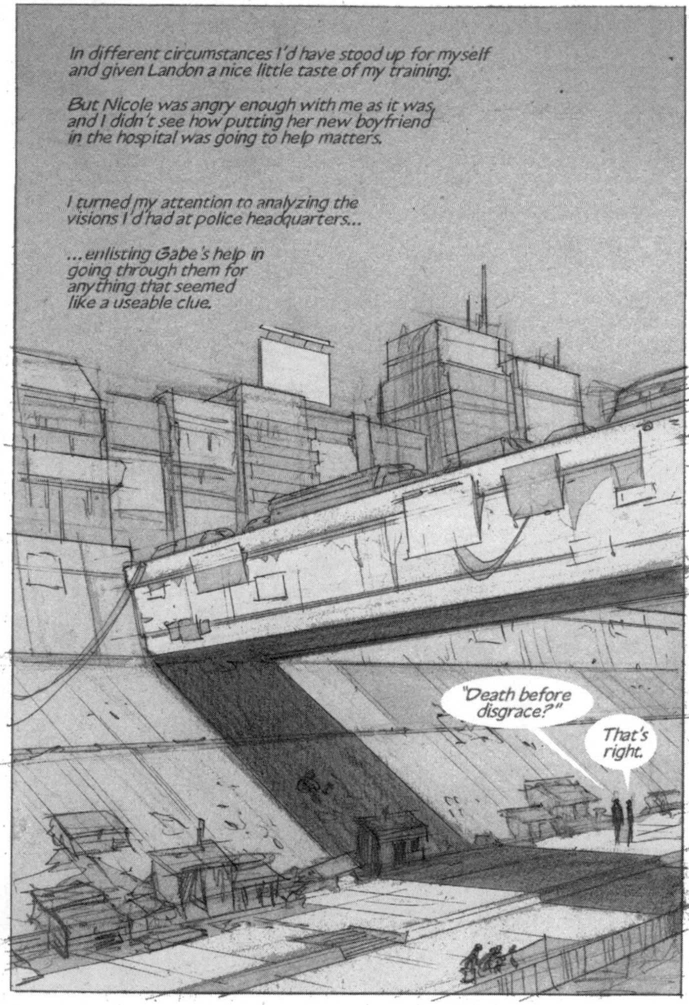
In different circumstances I'd have stood up for myself and given Landon a nice little taste of my training.
But Nicole was angry enough with me as it was, and I didn't see how putting her new boyfriend in the hospital was going to help matters.
I turned my attention to analyzing the visions I'd had at police headquarters...
...enlisting Gabe's help in going through them for anything that seemed like a useable clue.
"Death before disgrace?"
That's right.

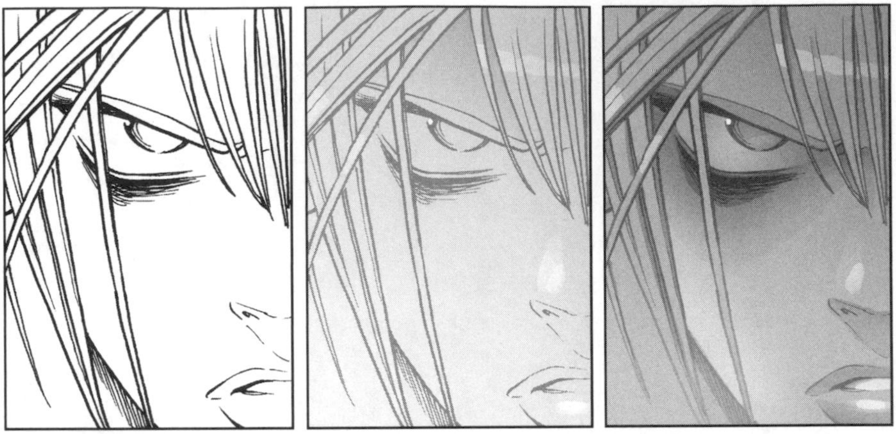

From the very beginning of my career I have been fascinated by the effects that are achieved when one adds gray tones to pen and ink illustrations. Though I generally minimize the toning on Talia, I felt this moment in the story called for an added sense of three-dimensionality.

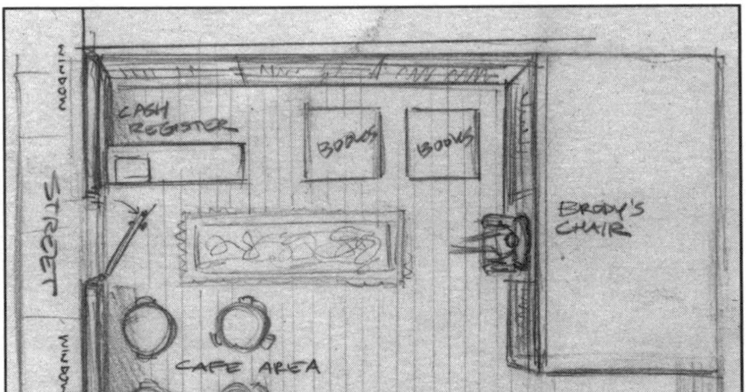
CASH REGISTER
BOOKS
BOOKS
BRODY'S CHAIR
STREET
CAFE AREA

It took some thinking to devise a situation in which Brody would-- though doing nothing wrong-- appear to break Landon's rule about stalking Nicole. Once I came up with the bookstore idea, I needed to lay out a floor plan so that Brody would be in just the right place when Nicole opened the door.

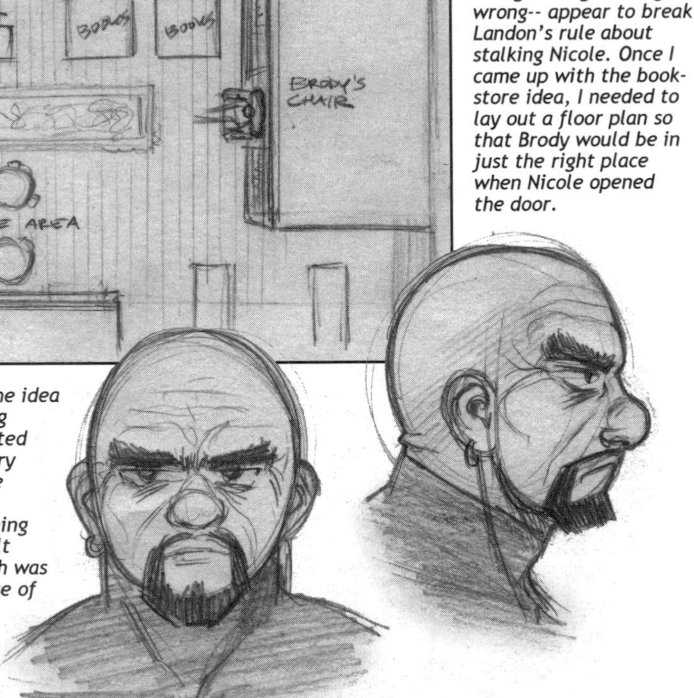

I briefly toyed with the idea of Landon's men being drawn in an exaggerated style, one of them very round-headed and the other thin and lanky. Once I got into sketching out the sequence I felt the cartoony approach was undercutting the sense of danger I needed the scene to convey.

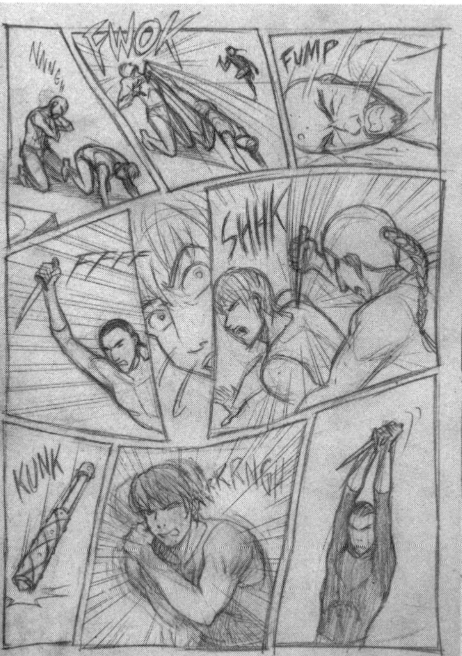
FWOK
FUMP
SHHK
KUNK

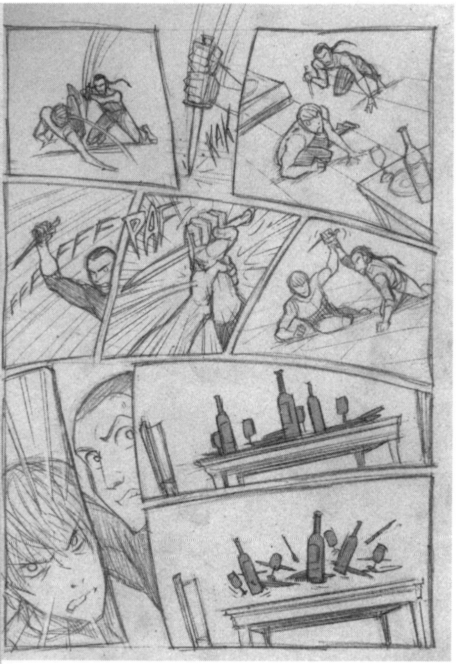
KAK
RAF

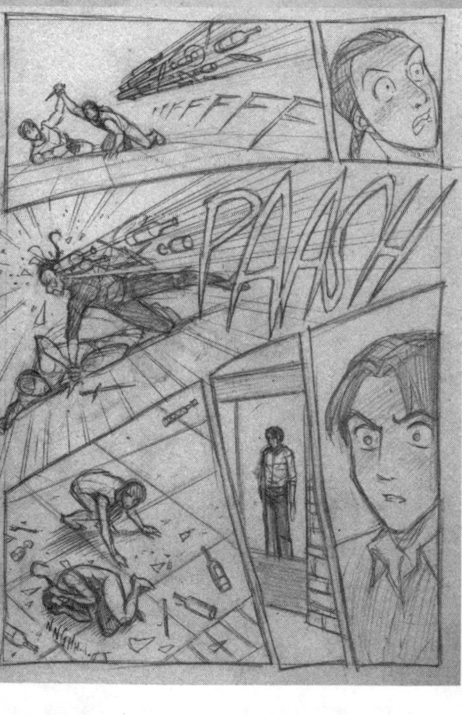

There had been no fight scene in the story since the end of book two, so I wanted to make sure this one really delivered. I planned out every step of it as one might for a film.

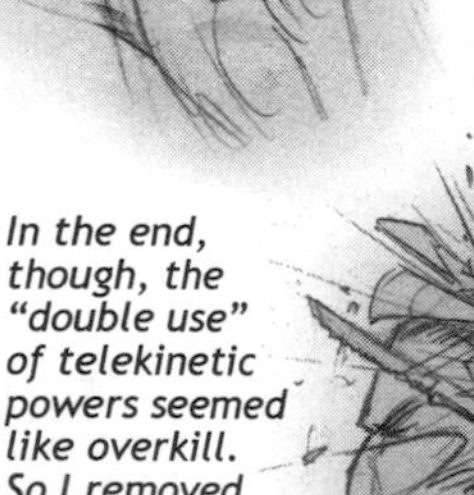

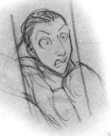

It was originally going to be several pages longer, with Brody getting stabbed in the shoulder and using his telekinetic powers to send bottles and plates flying through the air.

In the end, though, the "double use" of telekinetic powers seemed like overkill. So I removed the whole sequence to tighten things up and move the fight along to its finish.

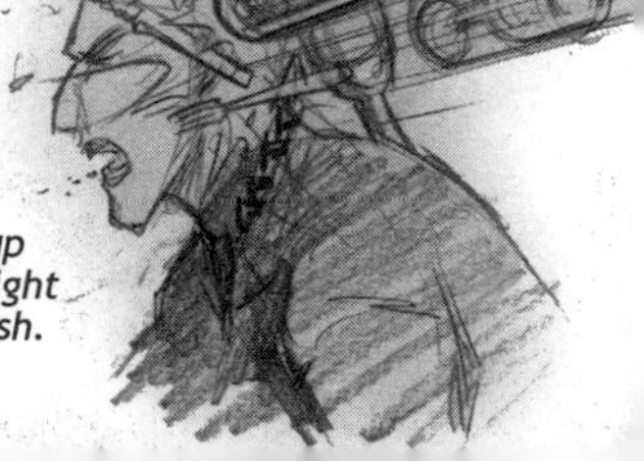

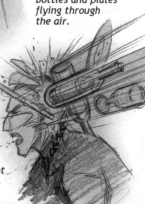

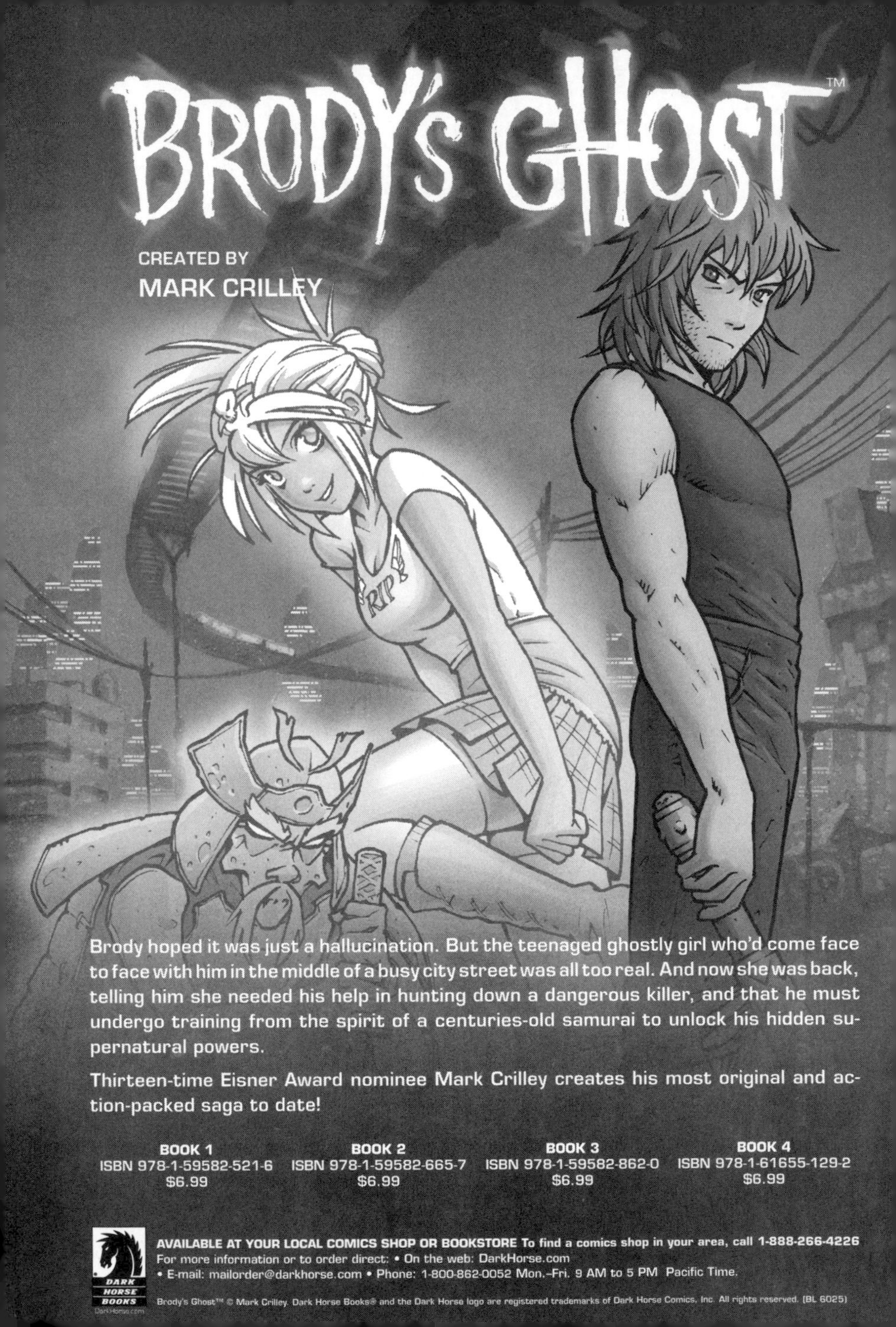

BRODY'S GHOST™
CREATED BY
MARK CRILLEY
RIP

Brody hoped it was just a hallucination. But the teenaged ghostly girl who'd come face to face with him in the middle of a busy city street was all too real. And now she was back, telling him she needed his help in hunting down a dangerous killer, and that he must undergo training from the spirit of a centuries-old samurai to unlock his hidden supernatural powers.

Thirteen-time Eisner Award nominee Mark Crilley creates his most original and action-packed saga to date!

BOOK 1	BOOK 2	BOOK 3	BOOK 4
ISBN 978-1-59582-521-6	ISBN 978-1-59582-665-7	ISBN 978-1-59582-862-0	ISBN 978-1-61655-129-2
$6.99	$6.99	$6.99	$6.99

AVAILABLE AT YOUR LOCAL COMICS SHOP OR BOOKSTORE To find a comics shop in your area, call 1-888-266-4226
For more information or to order direct: • On the web: DarkHorse.com
• E-mail: mailorder@darkhorse.com • Phone: 1-800-862-0052 Mon.–Fri. 9 AM to 5 PM Pacific Time.

DARK HORSE BOOKS
DarkHorse.com

FINDER

CARLA SPEED McNEIL

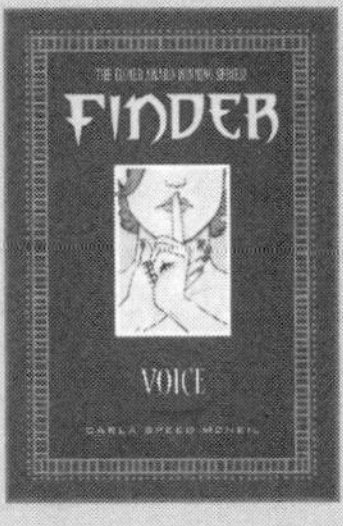
FINDER
VOICE
CARLA SPEED McNEIL

FINDER: VOICE

ISBN 978-1-59582-651-0
$19.99

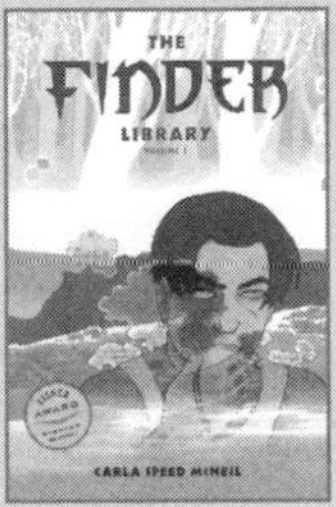
THE
FINDER
LIBRARY
CARLA SPEED McNEIL

THE FINDER LIBRARY VOLUME 1

ISBN 978-1-59582-652-7
$24.99

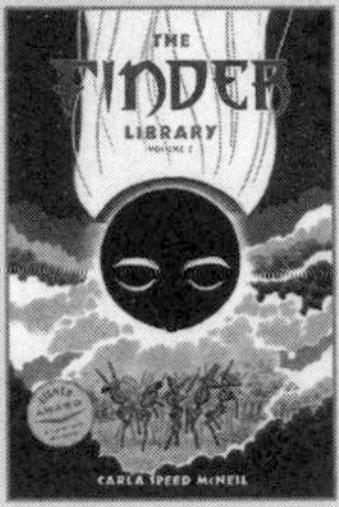
THE
FINDER
LIBRARY
CARLA SPEED McNEIL

THE FINDER LIBRARY VOLUME 2

ISBN 978-1-59582-653-4
$24.99

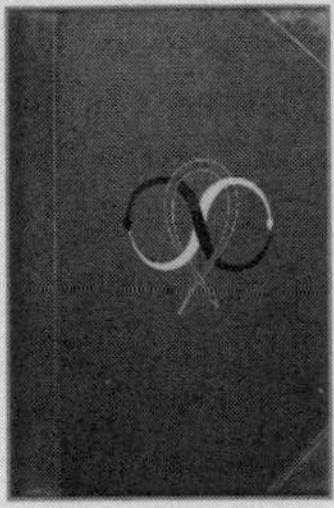

FINDER: TALISMAN
Special edition hardcover

ISBN 978-1-61655-027-1
$19.99

LOSE YOURSELF IN A WORLD BEYOND YOUR WILDEST DREAMS . . .

Since 1996, *Finder* has set the bar for science-fiction storytelling, with a lush, intricate world and compelling characters. Now, Dark Horse is proud to present Carla Speed McNeil's groundbreaking series in newly revised, expanded, affordablypriced volumes!

Follow enigmatic hero Jaeger through a "glorious, catholic pileup of high-tech SF, fannish fantasy, and street-level culture clash" (*Village Voice*), and discover the lush world and compelling characters that have carved *Finder* a permanent place in the pantheon of independent comics.

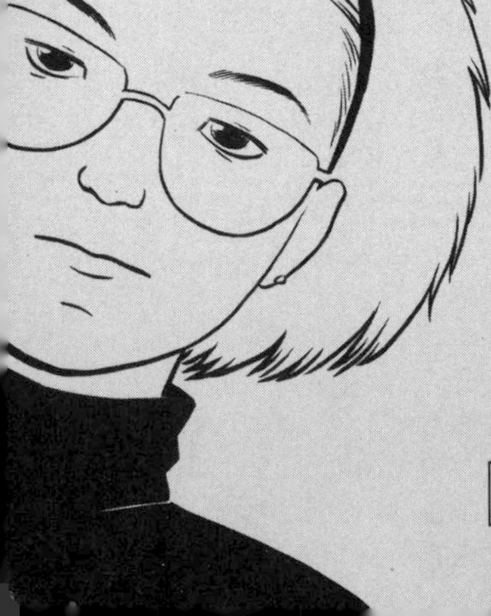

To find a comics shop in your area, call 1-888-266-4226
For more information or to order direct: On the web: DarkHorse.com
E-mail: mailorder@darkhorse.com
Phone: 1-800-862-0052
Mon–Fri 9 AM to 5 PM Pacific Time

DARK HORSE COMICS®
DarkHorse.com